LABORATORY EXPERIMENTS
FOR
MICROPROCESSOR SYSTEMS

John Crane

PRENTICE—HALL, INC. Englewood Cliffs, New Jersey 07632

Library of Congress Cataloging in Publication Data

Crane, John
   Laboratory experiments for microprocessor systems.

   1. Microprocessors -- Laboratory manuals. 2. Intel
8080 (Computer)--Laboratory manuals. I. Title.
QA76.5.C69   001.64'04'076   80-13173
ISBN 0-13-519694-9

Printed in the United States of America

10 9 8 7 6 5 4 3 2 1

Prentice-Hall International, Inc., London
Prentice-Hall of Australia Pty. Limited, Sydney
Prentice-Hall of Canada, Ltd., Toronto
Prentice-Hall of India Private Limited, New Delhi
Prentice-Hall of Japan, Inc., Tokyo
Prentice-Hall of Southeast Asia Pte. Ltd., Singapore
Whitehall Books Limited, Wellington, New Zealand

CONTENTS

PREFACE

This laboratory manual is written to provide an introduction to microprocessors. It covers hardware details and relationships of the basic elements that make up a typical microprocessor system. Because of its popularity, the 8080 was chosen as the microprocessor to guide the writing details of each experiment. Designed to follow and implement James W. Coffron's UNDERSTANDING AND TROUBLESHOOTING THE MICROPROCESSOR, the experiments in this manual are written around topics and functions that are typical of all microprocessor systems. This approach makes the experiments suitable for use in any hardware-oriented laboratory on microprocessor systems, regardless of the textbook that may be used to provide essential lecture and theory material.

The recent spectacular growth in numbers and applications of microprocessor-based digital systems has brought a new urgency to understanding exactly how such systems work. For those who will deal with these systems on a hardware level the foremost question is, "How do I learn what I need to know about microprocessor systems in order to work with them?"

This question must be answered on two levels: First, the theory level and, second, the practical hardware level. Usually, a textbook is selected to cover the theory of organization of microprocessor systems, elements that make up the system, how they relate to each other functionally, and how to program the system in order to use it. Such a procedure is useful as far as it goes, but it cannot and does not satisfy the needs of the troubleshooter, the technician, or anyone who must deal with microprocessor systems on a practical hardware level. Here, hands-on experience with hardware itself is an absolute essential: there simply is no satisfactory substitute. This laboratory manual has been carefully designed and written to meet this need.

ORGANIZATION OF THIS LABORATORY MANUAL

The basic organization of this laboratory manual has been carefully planned to conform to sound rules to learning. That is, wherever possible throughout the manual each step and each explanation is chosen to take advantage of, and build on, the reader's previously acquired knowledge and understanding.

Every effort is made to ensure that the reader will be able to understand and execute the operations that form the topic of focus and nucleus of each experiment. To that end, each experiment is page-referenced to the textbook UNDERSTANDING AND TROUBLESHOOTING THE MICROPROCESSOR, each experiment begins with a capsule summary and explanation of important information, each experiment presents a clear set of objectives to be achieved, each experiment employs both figures and text to enhance and maximize understanding, and each experiment represents a steady progression from what is known to what is new. In short, the objectives of each experiment <u>are</u> <u>achievable</u>. This serves as a great confidence builder as the mystery of microprocessors is steadily disspelled.

The study of microprocessors is much easier when we recognize and take advantage of one basic fact: a microprocessor system is a collection of hardware that is stable in one or the

other of two basic states, logical 1 or logical 0; when operating, the system switches from one static state to the other in
rapid succession. In the actual circuitry of a microprocessor
system these two basic states are represented by two different
voltage levels.

Now, if we can develop a way to apply and hold a logical 1
(or a logical 0) voltage for as long as we choose or need at the
point of signal origin, then we can check for proper voltages at
all points along the signal path from the point of origin to its
destination point. Moreover, the voltage can be checked with
inexpensive instruments such as a logic probe or a DC voltmeter.
This is the basic premise of static stimulus testing. The value
to the beginning troubleshooter of being able to have time to
trace signal paths and verify and learn "what should be there"
at each point in a system is incalculable.

The experiments in this manual assume that the user will
acquire or construct a Static Stimulus Tester.* This instrument
is inexpensive to build, and serves as both a valuable learning
tool and as an effective troubleshooting aid later. By the use
of this instrument one is able to realize the very real advantages that static techniques have to offer. Because it permits
a beginning microprocessor troubleshooter to set a logic level
and hold it for as long as needed, it is unparalleled in aiding
the understanding of microprocessor system organization, logic
paths, as well as the details of hardware operation. This approach provides a unique means of learning "what should be

_____

*Available from Creative Microprocessor Systems, Post
Office Box 1538, Los Gatos, California 95030

there" from the very beginning, while building a solid base of information plus techniques for effective troubleshooting that can be called upon often in the years ahead.

The fact is that every single memory cell, every operation, and every signal path of a microprocessor system must be checked before it can be said with confidence that a system will work properly. Even if sophisticated automatic test equipment is used to go through the steps of the checking process, the operator or someone must know that system organization and those signal paths well enough to pinpoint the trouble points when they occur and repair or correct them. Even if a troubleshooter comes to microprocessors with a software rather than a hardware background, one's introduction to microprocessor system hardware will be easier and the progress in understanding more rapid when using static techniques rather than dynamic techniques, in which the system is switching logic levels at kilohertz to megahertz speeds.

In this easy to follow manual, experiments 1 through 10 are devoted to the various aspects of hardware organization and the details of circuit operation using the static stimulus testing technique. At the conclusion of Experiment 10 the reader should be able to perform basic system operations, check to verify their proper execution, and locate the trouble site if the system fails to execute a command properly.

Experiments 11 through 18 are designed to develop an ability to write elementary programs and to expand on one's understanding and appreciation of the 1-to-1 relationship between hardware operation and program steps.

Experiments 19 and 20 focus on the troubleshooting of memories and I/O ports. Experiment 21 specializes in the effective use of the oscilloscope to examine and analyze the dynamic address, data, and control signals when a microprocessor system is in operation. Specific data sheets, schematics and other helpful information are included in the appendices which provide important information for the professional microprocessor technician.

The writing and preparation of this manual has involved the efforts of a group of people. In particular, I would like to thank Bill Long for his patient guidance, Kathy Wissig for all the keystrokes, Jim Coffron for his technical and moral support, and especially my wife, Alison, for going an extra mile. Beyond this there is my daughter, Charlotte, who at 8 months taste-tested every page of the manuscript.

John Crane
Palo Alto, California

INSTRUMENTS AND MATERIALS

Description of Item	Quantity
8080 microprocessor training system	12
Static Stimulus Tester (Creative Microprocessor Systems)	12
DC Volt-Ohmmeter	12
Logic probe	12
Current probe	12
TTL Data Book (Texas Instruments, Inc.)	12
MCS-80 User's Manual (Intel Corp., 1977), or MCS-80/85 Family User's Manual (Intel Corp., 1979)	12
DC power supply, 5 volt	12
Oscilloscope, dual-trace	6-12

This list of instruments and materials is based on a class size of 24 students. While a ratio of 1 student to 1 equipment set-up is ideal, costs may be a deterring factor. Experience in classes and seminars has shown the 2 student team to be workable, even exhibiting some positive elements. For one, the opportunity to cooperate and consult together when questions arise often produces answers from the students themselves, without requiring aid from the instructor. This is desirable, for it leads to an atmosphere of independence and self teaching, of self reliance and looking inward for solutions first. Also, the

2 student unit permits a trade-off which frees one member to concentrate on literature, specifications and documentation while his partner operates the hardware, makes measurements, and accumulates data.

EXPERIMENT 1
SYSTEM FAMILIARIZATION

<u>DISCUSSION</u>

In Experiment 1, we examine the make up of a typical microprocessor system: that is, we look at the functional block diagram, the integrated circuits (ICs) used, the function of each IC, the locations of the various ICs in the system and the source where data and specifications about each IC can be found. This is general "must have" information for anyone who works with microprocessors. Some of this information, such as the device's physical location on a printed circuit (PC) board, varies from system to system; however, these actual locations <u>must</u> be found before meaningful measurements can be taken and before work on the hardware can be done.

In the experiments that follow we shall look closely at which ICs are involved in each particular subsystem and operation that takes place in a microprocessor system.

In order to have a common starting point, let us look at the functional blocks that make up a typical microprocessor system. The microprocessor, or Central Processing Unit (CPU), is generally regarded as the center of the system, while the other functional units are usually referred to as peripherals, or subsystems. This simple system is shown in Figure 1-1.

As we examine each functional subsystem or peripheral one at a time in later experiments, we will become familiar with "what should be there" in terms of the devices, the circuit organization, the logic levels, and the signal or data paths. Our goal in Lab 1 is to do some preliminary work that will provide the basic information needed for the 20 experiments that follow.

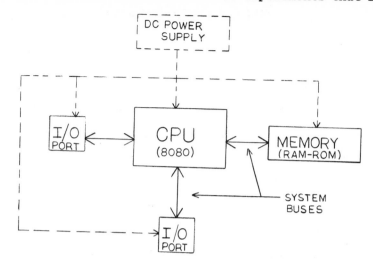

FIGURE 1-1   Functional block diagram of a microprocessor system

OBJECTIVES

    1.   To identify the major elements that make up a typical microprocessor system

    2.   To identify and find, using hardware and paper documentation, the physical location of all ICs used in the microprocessor system

    3.   To identify and make note of the sources of information about each IC for easy reference later

    4.   To identify the different classes of IC logic blocks that make up a total system and understand where each block is located, and

    5.   To practice locating relevant data and specifications, using the manufacturers' data sheets.

INSTRUMENTS AND MATERIALS

    1   8080 microprocessor training system

1   TTL data book

1   MCS-80 User's Manual (Intel Corp. 1977)

Note: If the MCS-80 User's Manual is not available,
            use the MCS-80/85 Family User's Manual (Intel
            Corp., 1979) or an equivalent. Referenced
            page and chapter numbers will need to be
            corrected.

Recommended Reading: UNDERSTANDING AND TROUBLESHOOTING
                        THE MICROPROCESSOR (referred to
                        hereafter as "Reference 1") by
                        James W. Coffron, Prentice Hall
                        1980, Pages 1-33

PROCEDURE

Step 1

1.1   If these are not already provided or available,
make a complete sketch of your system following the pattern of
Figure 1-2. List the manufacturers part number for each IC, the
function of the part (from manufacturers data sheets), and the
page number in the data reference book so that the part information can be looked up easily later.

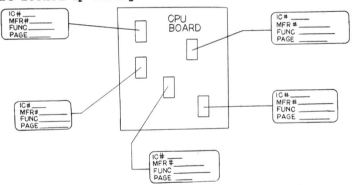

FIGURE 1-2   Partial block diagram of a microprocessor system showing physical
locations of ICs on the PC board

Step 2

2.1   Classify all of the ICs according to the functional group to which they belong. This gives one a review of
the digital elements (with which you are already familiar) that
make up a microprocessor system.   A suggested format for this

step is given in Table 1-1.

TABLE 1-1   Summary of system Integrated Circuits

Part Number	Page Reference	Supply Voltages Required	Notes and Comments
NAND gates 1. 2.			
Hex Inverters 1. 2.			
AND gates 1. 2.			
Bit Comparators 1. 2.			
Multivibrators 1. 2.			
Line Buffers 1. 2.			
Flip Flops 1. 2.			
Counters 1. 2.			
Memories 1.			

NOTE: Any additional functional devices in your system should be added to this table.

1.   What voltage (or voltages) does your DC power supply provide?

2.   Referring to the data collected in Step 2, how does the voltage required by the various ICs conform to the voltage available from the power supply? Are there any important differences?

3.   Other than the Central Processing Unit, did you find any digital functions with which you are not familiar?

4.   What logic families (TTL, CMOS, NMOS, etc.) are used in the ICs of your system?

5.   How well did this experiment fulfill its five objectives? Were there any shortcomings?

EXPERIMENT 2
INTRODUCTION TO
THE STATIC STIMULUS TESTER (SST)

DISCUSSION

The Static Stimulus Tester (SST) represents a unique tool for the investigation of microprocessor systems. The fundamental advantage of the SST is that it simplifies the complex, dynamic analysis of a microprocessor system into a straightforward static investigation. The demonstration and understanding of this instrument is the goal of this experiment.

When a microprocessor is commanding a system, it provides the proper logic levels and timing automatically; in this mode, the required combinations of logical voltage levels to read or write are held at logical 1 or logical 0 very briefly, usually just long enough to permit the read or write function to take place. The fleeting nature of such short duration logic pulses when the microprocessor is in command presents a number of difficulties and uncertainties in circuit testing and troubleshooting.

In static stimulus testing the SST takes the place of the microprocessor that is used in the system. Now you, the operator, become the microprocessor and you send out the correctly timed, proper logic levels on the right bus lines to the proper memory or other device pins to accomplish a memory read or write. To do this, the microprocessor is first removed from its socket. This permits outside access to all of the address, data, and control bus lines that are normally controlled by the microprocessor. To realize this access in the easiest and most effective way, the Static Stimulus Tester, a simple switch-controlled instrument with a suitable means of connection to the circuit under test, should be constructed or purchased. To operate, the SST is connected by a cord and plug (which fits into the vacated microprocessor socket) to the system being checked.

With the Static Stimulus Tester plugged into the microprocessor socket of the system, one can now send out a logical 1 or a logical 0 to any bus line one chooses, in any sequence one chooses. More importantly, the operator can hold the chosen logic level steady on any bus line as long as needed to check its progress to its destination point in any part of the system. Thus, it becomes an easy matter to check for short and open circuits, inoperative ICs, and faulty voltage levels in nearly every part of the system except the system clocks, which must be treated separately.

Figure A-7 (Appendix) shows the schematic for the SST. Notice that provisions are made for use with the 8080 and 8085 microprocessors. (Other microprocessors will require minor modifications to meet individual differences). Figure 2-1 shows the physical layout of the SST. Switches 1 and 2 allow the selection of address words that are routed to the system address bus. Switch 3 selects the data words that are sent out on the bi-directional data bus. ICs 3 and 4 provide tri-state buffering to the data bus. Any data that is active on the data bus is buffered by ICs 5, 6, 7, and 8 and displayed by light emitting diodes (LEDs) at the outputs of these buffers. The following signals are generated by switches 4, 5, 6, and 7:

SST	8080	8085	DESCRIPTION
BIN/$\overline{\text{RD}}$	DBIN	$\overline{\text{RD}}$	Data Bus Enable
$\overline{\text{WR}}$	$\overline{\text{WR}}$	$\overline{\text{WR}}$	Write Signal
SYNC/ALE	SYNC	ALE	8080: Strobe Status Word; 8085: Strobe Memory Address (A_{15}-A_0)
IO/$\overline{\text{M}}$		IO/$\overline{\text{M}}$	IO or Memory Select

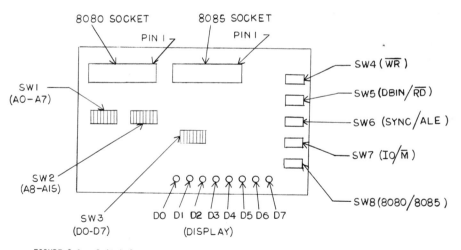

FIGURE 2-1   Switch layout and IC positions of the Static Stimulus Tester (SST)

These four signals are the control signals that normally originate internally in the 8080 and 8085 microprocessors.

Another advantage of approaching microprocessor systems in

a static mode is that it greatly aids in learning what the logic paths are for each operation, that is, for writing to and reading from memory, for communicating with input/output ports (I/O) and for controlling the various functions of the system. If we are to deal effectively with a microprocessor system on the practical hardware level, we must know "what should be there" at important points in the system. This experiment introduces the concept of static stimulus testing; future experiments show exactly how to use it effectively. So, what are we waiting for? Let's get started!

OBJECTIVES

1. To learn how the static stimulus tester is organized and gain familiarity with the operating controls, and

2. To practice tracing signals within the SST from the schematic: to verify the 1-to-1 relationship between logic levels (voltages) at the output plug terminals and at the switch positions.

INSTRUMENTS AND MATERIALS

1   Static Stimulus Tester (SST)

1   Logic probe or DC voltmeter

1   DC power supply

Recommended Reading: Reference 1
                            Pages 212-222

PROCEDURE

Step 1

1.1   Apply power to the SST (+5 volts and ground). Set the 8080/8085 switch to the 8080 position.

1.2   Toggle on and off the individual switches of DIP SW3 that control the data bus lines D_7-D_0. Verify visually that each switch controls one corresponding LED.

1.3   With a DC voltmeter or logic probe, verify that toggling the switch for line D_7 varies the logical voltage from 1 to 0 on bus D_7 at the 8080 socket pin 6, as well as turning on and off the LED on line D_7. Repeat this procedure for each data bus line, checking for proper logic voltage at appropriate 8080 socket pins (see schematic) until all data bus lines D_7-D_0 and all LEDs have been checked for correct logical voltage levels.

1.4   If your SST has provision for use with the 8085 microprocessor, set the 8080/8085 switch in the 8085 position. Now, toggle the individual switches of S3 and proceed to check visually all LEDs, using the DC voltmeter or logic probe, check all data bus lines D_7-D_0 at the 8080 socket (pins 12-19). Do this in the same way you did in Steps 1.2 and 1.3 for the 8080 socket. When all checks have been completed successfully, you have now verified proper operation and control of all data bus lines within the SST.

Step 2

2.1   Now, we turn our attention to the address bus lines, A_{15}-A_0. Note that these lines are not monitored by LEDs so our checks will be for proper logic voltage levels at the 8080/8085 socket pins only.

First, set the 8080/8085 switch to the 8080 position. Then, toggle the individual switch for A_0 on SW1. At the same time, check the DC logic voltage level on bus line A_0 at pin 25 of the 8080 socket. If the voltage changes from logical 1 to logical 0 when the switch is toggled, the circuit is operating normally.

Repeat this check for address lines A_{15}-A_0 to verify that all address lines are operating normally.

2.2   Set the 8080/8085 switch to the 8085 position. Repeat the checks just made in Step 2.1 on all address lines connected to the 8085 socket (A_{15}-A_8) to verify that all of these lines are operating correctly.

2.3   Check all control lines, SYNC, DBIN, and $\overline{WR}$ on the 8080 socket and IO/$\overline{M}$, ALE, $\overline{WR}$ and $\overline{RD}$ on the 8085 socket. Verify that switches 4 to 7 govern the logic levels on these control signal buses. When you have completed these checks and found no pin or LED that failed to toggle when the controlling switch was changed, the SST is operating normally and ready for use.

QUESTIONS

1. When the switch on address line A_8 is <u>open</u> what is the logic voltage level on address line A_8? _____. On 8080 socket pin 34? _____.

2. When the switch on line A_6 is <u>closed</u> what is the logic voltage level on address line A_6? _____. What is the number of the socket pin that this line is connected to on the 8080 socket? _____. On the 8085 socket? _____.

3. Make a list of the ICs used in the Static Stimulus Tester, their function, and the page reference in the data book where complete specifications can be found.

4. How well did this experiment fulfill our original objectives? Were there any shortcomings?

EXPERIMENT 3
SYSTEM BUSES: THE 3-BUS ARCHITECTURE

DISCUSSION

A prominent feature that is common to 8-bit microprocessor systems is 3-bus architecture. This describes the organization and uses of communication paths within the system. That is, lines (wires, PC board traces) with similar functions are grouped together as a "bus" and designated according to what they do. Thus, we have an address bus, a data bus and a control bus. The 8080 microprocessor has connections, or pin terminals, for 16 address lines (A_{15}-A_0) that compose the address bus, 8 data lines (D_7-D_0) that make up the data bus, and a 5-signal control bus* to direct the system functions. For the 8080 microprocessor the control bus is made up of the following signals:

SIGNAL NAME	PRONOUNCED
$\overline{\text{MEMR}}$	Memory Read Bar
$\overline{\text{MEMW}}$	Memory Write Bar
$\overline{\text{I/OR}}$	Input/Output Read Bar
$\overline{\text{I/OW}}$	Input/Output Write Bar

Any microprocessor that serves as the CPU of a system routinely communicates with a number of peripheral elements. Examples are memory (ROM, RAM) and I/O ports. The number of peripherals varies from system to system. This means that each

---

*The 8080 has provision for an interrupt acknowledge bar signal (INTA) which will not be used at this time.

12

of the three buses that originate at the microprocessor pins go to several different terminations, or points of use. More specifically, each address line, each data line, and each control line has a "load" that consists of several parallel elements. This is illustrated in Figure 3-1.

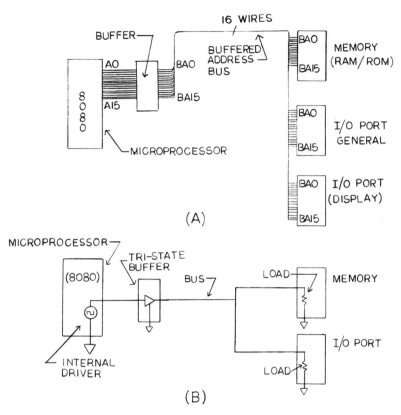

FIGURE 3-1 (A) Basic physical make-up of a typical address bus structure. (B) Basic electrical arrangement of bus lines going to several destination points in parallel

The fact that the load on each bus line is composed of parallel elements has important implications: First, a short circuit or excessive load in any element shows up as a short on the entire line; second, the total current the source must furnish is the sum of the currents drawn by all parallel ele-

13

ments connected to that particular line. Third, if the micro-processor is to communicate with only one element at a time, the other elements must be turned off and placed in a high impedance (tri-state) condition; that is, only the desired communication paths or functions should be enabled if the system is to operate normally.

Frequently, the amount of current the microprocessor can supply is not enough to satisfy all of the parallel load elements that are connected to a particular line or bus. In this case a buffer, or current amplifier, is added to increase the drive capability of the microprocessor. Sometimes multiplexers or other devices serve this purpose in addition to their other roles in the system. The use of buffering is standard practice in most systems; look for it, and expect it. Such devices actually are in series with the signal line, representing intervening hardware between the origination point, or source, and the destination point, or point of use of digital signal information. After buffering, address line A_0 is usually designated BA_0, MA_0, or in some other fashion to distinquish it from the unbuffered line. Data lines are treated similarly.

This experiment introduces the 3-bus architecture common to microprocessor systems and discusses some of the physical and electrical characteristics you should expect to find when dealing with the actual hardware of an operating system. In the course of the experiment you are asked to make sketches and measurements, because these skills are needed for systematic, practical troubleshooting.

OBJECTIVES

    1. To become acquainted with the physical aspects of 3-bus architecture by examining a working microprocessor system, and

    2. To become familiar with the typical electrical organization and bus structure of 8-bit microprocessor systems, and to review the implications of parallel circuits as they apply to 3-bus architecture.

INSTRUMENTS AND MATERIALS

1   8080 microprocessor training system

1   Volt-ohmmeter (VOM) or other instrument capable
    of measuring ohms and DC volts
    Schematics, manufacturers specifications, data books
    and pertinent literature

    Recommended Reading: Your 8080 System Manual

PROCEDURE

Step 1

We shall look first at the schematic of the CMS training system, which is shown in Figures A-1 to A-6 of the Appendix, then at the system you are working with, if it is different.

    1.1   Look closely at the schematics of Figures A-1 to A-6. From these schematics, make a sketch similar to Figure 3-1 showing the different points and parallel elements connected to the lines of the address bus of the CMS Trainer. On your sketch, identify each of these parallel elements as closely as you can (IC number, manufacturer's device number, and function). Also show any buffering devices.

1.2   If your system is different, repeat Step 1.1 for the system you are working with. How does your system compare with the CMS system's address bus?

1.3   Look closely at the data bus on the schematics of Figures A-1 to A-6. Make a sketch similar to Figure 3-1 showing the different parallel circuits connected to the lines of the data bus. Identify each parallel element as closely as you can (IC number, manufacturer's device number and function). Include on your sketch any buffering devices found.

1.4   If your system is different from our example system, repeat the procedure followed in Step 1.3 for the system you are working with. How does the data bus of your system compare with that of the CMS system?

1.5   Examine and make sketches of the control bus in the same manner as you did for the address and data buses. Note that each line of the control bus carries a particular signal, and hence tends to be more uniquely routed than the individual lines of the address bus and the data bus. How does the control bus of your system compare with that of the CMS system in this step?

Step 2

Referring to schematics, in Step 1 we examined and compared drawings of bus structures, buffering, and parallel load elements that are characteristic of the 3-bus architecture of microprocessor systems. Now, let us relate our sketches to the actual system, because we need to see how a schematic and functional block diagram compares to the physical location and layout of the working hardware.

16

2.1   Look closely at the hardware of your microprocessor system and at the functional sketches you made from
schematics in Step 1.1. Locate the actual, physical source
point (the microprocessor) of the address lines, the buffers,
and the parallel load elements you identified in your earlier
sketch. Now, make a new sketch similar to Figure 3-2, to show
the actual physical location of each element on the PC board of
your system. On each element indicate the device pin numbers
for each address line that is connected.

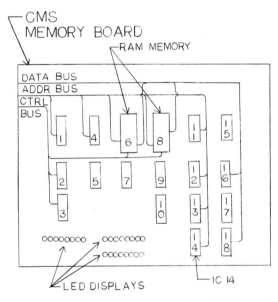

FIGURE 3-2   Physical layout of the memory board of the CMS training system
showing bus interconnections. For expanded details showing individual bus
lines, IC numbers, and device pin numbers, refer to FIGURE A-4A and A-4B.

2.2   To verify the correctness of the sketch you just
made, connect the "Common", or ground, lead of your ohmmeter to
the microprocessor pin or buffer output pin that connects to the
address line A_0 or BA_0. Now, measure the resistance of address
line A_0 or BA_0 between the microprocessor or buffer and the pin
of every parallel element to which A_0 or BA_0 is connected. Is

17

the resistance large or small? Is your measured value the amount of resistance that should be there? Does the resistance change when the ohmmeter leads are reversed (+/- becomes -/+)?

2.3   For practice, and to develop skill and speed, repeat the resistance measurements of the last step until the resistance of all address lines (A_7-A_0) has been checked. Do all of the address lines show direct connections as indicated in the original schematic and your sketches?

2.4   Now, look closely at the data lines. Sketch the physical location of all elements connected to the data lines, including buffers, similar to the sketch just made of the address lines. Put appropriate device pin numbers on your sketch to show exactly where each line connects to a particular device.

2.5   Verify the correctness of your sketch of the data lines by measuring the resistance of each line between the microprocessor or buffer output and the input pins of the parallel elements that are connected to it. How much resistance do you expect (approximately)? How do the resistance values of the data lines compare with those of the address lines?

2.6   Look closely at the control lines and the sketch make in Step 1.3. Sketch the physical location of all elements connected to the control lines. On your sketch, indicate device pin numbers to which each line is connected.

2.7   Verify the correctness of your sketch of the control lines by measuring the resistance of each line between the microprocessor or buffer and all parallel elements to which the line is connected.

Step 3

If any one of the elements in a parallel circuit develops a short circuit, or lower than normal resistance, that defect will appear as a short at all points along the circuit. In this final step of Experiment 3, we investigate this aspect of microprocessor structure and parallel circuit behavior.

3.1.   Select a particular address line or data line for experimentation. Introduce a short circuit by connecting the input pin of one of the parallel load elements (to which the selected address line is connected) to ground via a wire or clip lead. Now, connect the common lead of the ohmmeter to ground, and, using the other lead, measure the resistance between ground and all of the various points to which the shorted line is connected. Do they not all show a short circuit? How would one proceed to isolate such a problem?

3.2   Remove the short introduced in Step 3.1. Now, repeat the measurements just made. Do all points indicate the same value (not zero)? This measurement should show the normal value of resistance, unless an undetected problem still exists.

QUESTIONS

1.   What does the term "3-bus architecture" mean?

2.   The 8080 has pin terminals for how many address lines? Data lines?

3.   Do address, data, and control buses usually make direct connections between the microprocessor and its peripherals, or do these buses usually pass through other hardware in going between the microprocessor and a particular peripheral element? Explain.

4.   How can one find out exactly where an address, data, or control line begins and terminates (device, location and pin number) on a particular microprocessor system that sits in front of him or her?

5.   How will a shorted data bus input line to an I/O port or memory affect the operation of that line where a different destination (I/O port or other peripheral element) is concerned? Explain why.

6.   Describe how one might troubleshoot and find the fault site in an open address line, data line, or control line.

EXPERIMENT 4
WRITING DATA TO MEMORY
AND READING DATA FROM MEMORY

DISCUSSION

Writing data to memory is the process by which desired bits
are put into RAM memory, where they are stored for retrieval
later when the information that they represent is needed.
Reading data from memory is the process by which stored bits of
information are retrieved from RAM or ROM for use in the system.

Both writing data to memory and reading data from memory
require that the exact address (location in memory) be specified, as a first step. This is done by choosing the proper
address code, consisting of logical 1s (ones) and 0s (zeroes).
This series of 1s and 0s must be placed on the address bus, one
bit per line, at its point of origin or source. In normal
system operation, this source is the set of designated address
pins of the microprocessor; in our experiment, the source is the
set of switches on the Static Stimulus Tester (SST) which we set
manually to the proper address code and which connect to the
proper address lines. The memory is, of course, the destination
point of the information we have placed on the address lines at
the source.

In an 8080 based design, data placed on the address lines
at the microprocessor pins in a memory write operation should
appear at the memory pins immediately, unless something is
wrong. Other microprocessors handle this differently, but with
the 8080, if address line A_0 is toggled from 1 to 0 at the

21

microprocessor, line A_0 at the memory input should toggle from 1 to 0 simultaneously.

Next, the proper Status Word for a memory write operation must be placed on the data lines. The purpose of the Status Word is to prepare the memory to receive data from the data lines for storage, and to turn off or disable other parts of the system, such as I/O ports, that are not involved in a memory write operation. One might say that the Status Word "defines" the operation to be performed.

Status Words for the operations of the 8080 are found in a Status Word Chart provided by the device manufacturer (see Figure A-8 in the Appendix). Like the address information, the Status Word consists of logical 1s and 0s that are placed on the data bus by switches on the SST, which we can set manually to provide the correct bit for each data line. Following this, the Sync must be activated (logical 1 for the 8080 system) and then deactivated to latch the Status Word prior to the next step.

At this point, all is in readiness for the data we wish to store in memory; that is, after the address has been set to the desired location, the Status Word has defined the type of operation to be performed, and the Sync has latched the Status Word, we are ready to devote our attention to the data itself. Now, the desired data to be stored in the individual cells of memory must be placed on the individual lines of the data bus at its origin or source, just as the address bits were set. In normal operation, the source is the set of designated data pins of the microprocessor (D_7-D_0); in our experiment, the source will be the manually set switches of the SST, which are connected to the proper data bus lines.

22

Finally the write signal $\overline{\text{WR}}$ must be brought low (logical 0) and then high (logical 1) to accomplish the actual writing of data into the individual memory cells where it will be stored. This action completes the memory write operation.

To check on what is written in memory, it is necessary to perform a memory read operation.

Reading from memory with the 8080 system shares elements in common with writing data to memory; that is, the address to be read from must be set on the address lines in exactly the same way for a memory read as for a memory write operation. Next, the proper Status Word for a memory read is placed on the data lines to define the operation to be performed. Sync then latches the Status Word for a memory read operation. Finally, the DBIN signal is brought high to bring the data from memory to the microprocessor and complete the memory read operation. Fig-

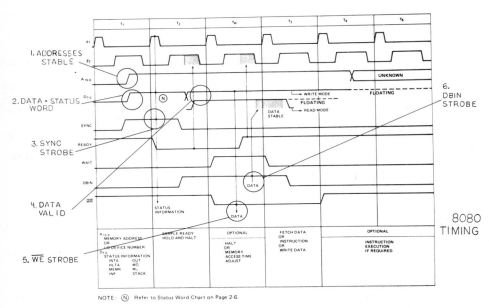

FIGURE 4-1 Derivation of steps for memory read and memory write operations from an actual 8080 timing diagram. See page 2-8 of the MCS-80 User's Manual.

ure 4-1 shows how the 8080 would execute memory read and write operations.

The address bus lines, data bus lines, and control bus lines do not usually connect directly from the source -- in this case, the microprocessor -- to the destination point, in this case, the memory. Typically, these lines include intervening hardware, buffers, decoders, and other devices, between the source point and the destination point of data. See Figure A-2 (Appendix). All of this intervening hardware must be turned on, or enabled, in order to complete the data path between the source point and the destination point. Different microprocessors provide for this in different ways. The point is, one should look for and expect to find intervening hardware between source points and destination points of data on the various bus lines.

As a practical matter, it is usually easy to identify the point of origin and the point of destination of signals. From there, one can trace the data path and identify hardware blocks that may be in it, no matter what system one is working with. When trouble occurs and data measured at the source point fails to reach the destination point, the troubleshooter must check each bit of intervening hardware to find out exactly what and where the fault is.

OBJECTIVES

1.   To learn and practice the details of writing data to memory in a microprocessor system

2.   To learn and practice the details of reading data from memory in a microprocessor system, and

3.   To have the experience of verifying the operational and technical details of a memory write and a memory read operation with actual hardware; to have the opportunity to make measurements of the system with diagnostic instruments; and to follow the data paths and logic levels in a properly operating system and see for oneself what should be there.

INSTRUMENTS AND MATERIALS

1   8080 microprocessor training system

1   DC voltmeter and/or logic probe

     TTL Data Book, MCS-80 User's Manual, pertinent

     literature as needed

              Recommended Reading: Reference 1
                                          Pages 35-52, 59-75,
                                          129-141

PROCEDURE

Step 1

The first goal is to write a selected data byte (8 bits of data) into a particular location in memory. To accomplish this, we do the following:

1.1   Suppose we choose to write the data 38_{16}* into memory location $00BB_{16}$. First, we must change the hexadecimal values into binary notation:

38_{16}(hexadecimal) = _____, the data in binary notation.

$00BB_{16}$(hexidecimal) = _____, the address in binary notation. (Upper byte = 00)

_____

   *38_{16} means 38 is a hexadecimal number, Base 16.

1.2   Set the individual switches of the SST that control the address lines (A_{15}-A_0) to equal the binary form of the address, as determined in Step 1.1 and illustrated in Figure 4-2A. See Figure 2-1 for a physical layout of the SST.

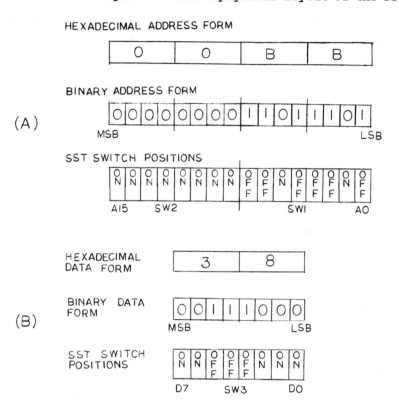

FIGURE 4-2   (A) and (B) Translation of address and data notations into actual Static Stimulus Tester switch positions

1.3   With a logic probe or DC voltmeter, check the voltage level on each address line A_7-A_0 to see if it falls within the legitimate boundaries that represent 1s and 0s as set by the address switches in Step 1.2. Do the voltages agree with the address that was set?

1.4   Set the individual switches of the SST that

26

control the data lines to the binary form of the Status Word for a memory write operation (status word = 00000000_2). D_7 to D_0 should now all be "off". See Figure 4-2B.

1.5　　　　Force the Sync signal high (logical 1). This is accomplished by setting SW6 of the SST to the logical 1 position. This should make pin 9, the control pin, of IC6 and IC14 on the CPU board of the CMS training system active. (Refer to Appendix, Figure A-3A). Check this with a logic probe or DC voltmeter to be certain that the Sync signal is indeed logical 1.

1.6　　　　Reset the Sync signal to 0. Check pin 9 of IC6 and IC14 again. It should no longer be active.

Note:　　Steps 1.1 through 1.3 specify the exact address we wish to write to in memory. Steps 1.4 through 1.6 define the operation as a memory write by choosing and implementing the correct Status Word for a memory write. At this point, the address is specified, the operation to be performed is defined, and the system is ready to receive the data we wish to store.

1.7.　　　　Now, set the individual switches that control the data lines to equal the binary form of the data 38_{16} as found in Step 1.1 and shown in Figure 4-2B. Check the data line voltages to see if they agree with the series of 1s and 0s you have just placed on the data lines.

1.8　　　　Set the $\overline{WR}$ switch to logical 0 (active low). This enables the memory to receive and store data.

1.9　　　　Return the $\overline{WR}$ switch to logical 1, which represents the inactive state. Now, no more data can enter the memory until the $\overline{WR}$ switch is again brought to active low position. This completes the write operation to memory.

Step 2

To write data to the next address in memory, Steps 1.3 through 1.9 could be repeated, changing only the specified address in Step 1.1 to BC_{16}. However, the Status Word is already latched in the system. Therefore, Steps 1.4 through 1.6 can be deleted. To write to the next location in memory, then, only the following steps are required.

2.1.   Set the address line switches A_7-A_0 to BC_{16}, the next address in memory to write. Check that the address has changed at the input pins of the memory (pins 1 through 7 and 21 of ICs 6 and 8 if the CMS trainer is being used) by measuring the logical voltage levels there.

2.2   Choose the data to be written to address BC_{16}, as an example, 27_{16}. Set the chosen data on the data lines as in Step 1.7. Check it as before, then proceed as in Steps 1.8 and 1.9 to complete the write operation in this second memory location. One could continue in this fashion until all desired data is written into memory, or until all memory locations have been filled.

Step 3

To read data from memory (to verify that the data we just wrote to memory is indeed stored and can be retrieved) we do the following in an 8080 system:

1.   Address bus = location in memory to read.

2.   Data bus = status word for memory read (82_{16}).

3.   Sync = high then low (1 then 0).

4.   DBIN = high (logical 1). Read data is now on the system data bus and displayed by the SST.

3.1   Perform the memory read procedure outlined above

for address 00BB$_{16}$ in memory. Verify that the data agrees with that specified in Step 1.1, 38$_{16}$. Because the status word for a memory read operation is now latched in the system any address in memory can be read by setting the address and enabling the DBIN signal.

3.2   Set the address on SW1 and SW2 on the SST to 00BC$_{16}$. Set DBIN high. Verify that the data bus now equals the data chosen in Step 2.2.

Step 4

To gain confidence in the procedures outlined in Steps 1 to 3, write and read the RAM locations specified in Table 4-1. If your system does not have RAM at these locations, make your own address choices.

TABLE 4-1   Data to be written to memory and read from memory. Show in both hexadecimal and binary form

ADDRESS (IN HEX)	WRITE DATA		READ DATA		NOTES
	HEX	BINARY	HEX	BINARY	
OC1A	OE				
OC1B	EF				
ED24	AA				
0056	AO				
0057	69				
1047	31				
0346	DA				
ABCD	BC				
0088	77				

Step 5

5.1   Make a functional block diagram of all ICs involved in a memory write and a memory read operation in your
trainer, similar to that of Figure 4-3.

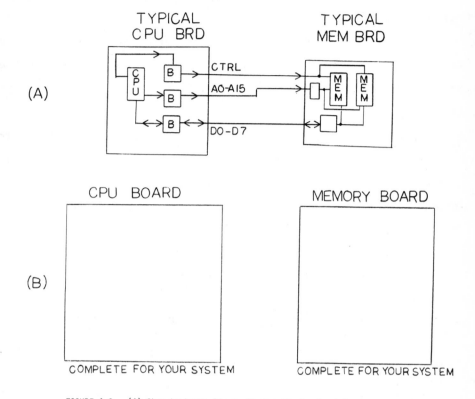

(A)

(B)

FIGURE 4-3   (A) Show by heavy lines all the ICs involved in a memory write
operation for your system. (B) Complete the diagrams and show by heavy lines
all the ICs involved in each operation of a memory read in your system.

QUESTIONS

1.   Could one determine the sequence of steps to be performed in order to accomplish a memory write operation by examining the timing diagram of Figure 4-1? Explain.

2.   How important is it to follow the specified sequence
of operations in a microprocessor system?

3.   When is it necessary to know the ICs and their pin

numbers in a microprocessor system? Give examples.

4.   When measuring a logical voltage level at a particular point in a microprocessor system, how does one know if the voltage indicated is what is supposed to be there?

5.   If the voltage at one of the device pins is not what should be there, list as many possible causes as you can think of.

6.   Referring to Question 5, how can one check out each of the possible trouble causes you have listed?

EXPERIMENT 5
WRITING DATA TO INPUT/OUTPUT (I/O) PORTS

DISCUSSION

In Experiment 4 we examined the events required for a microprocessor to store and retrieve data from any location in the system memory. With some minor modifications, these same events can be applied to the 8080 sytem to transport data to and from other destinations that represent the outside world through system input/output ports (I/O ports).

An input port is any device or group of circuitry through which a microprocessor can receive data from a source that is external to the system. Typical input ports are paper tape readers, keyboards and punched card readers. When the data that has entered the system via an input port has been processed by the system, the results of processing are communicated to the outside world through an external device. Such a device is called an output port. Typical of output ports are line-printers, LED displays, graphic plotters, and paper tape punches. If a particular device can both transmit and receive data from the system, it is called an input/output (I/O) port. Magnetic tape drives, hard and floppy disc drives, and terminals fall into this category.

In the following experiment, we will examine the use and configuration of typical I/O ports and see how the microprocessor communicates with them. We will use the term I/O port to describe either an input only, output only, or input/output combined port.

The number of I/O ports in a system varies greatly, depending on the application of the system. Regardless of the number

available, each port must be uniquely identified. This is neces-

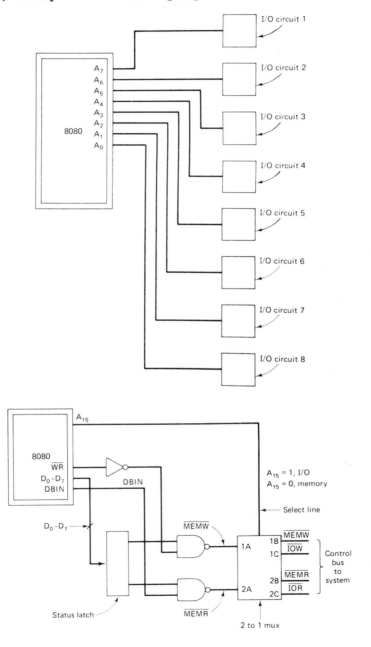

FIGURE 5-1   Typical I/O structures for an 8080 system. See Reference 1,
Chapter 5.

33

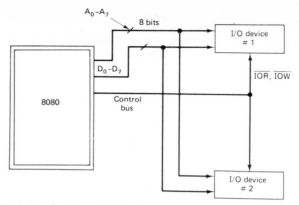

FIGURE 5-1 (continued) Typical I/O structure for an 8080 system.

sary because <u>all</u> of the ports are connected to the system data and address buses.

Figure 5-1 shows typical I/O structures of a microprocessor system. Just as each location in memory has a unique address, so each I/O port in a system has a unique address, usually called the select code of the port. In fact, in certain cases the I/O ports can be treated as if they are memory locations. This scheme is called memory mapped I/O.

Whether a microprocessor is performing an I/O read or an I/O write operation, it must go through a prescribed sequence of events. These events are performed at megahertz speeds in normal microprocessor system operation. However, there is no reason why the events could not occur in a very slow, static fashion, provided the prescribed sequence is followed. Therefore, we will use the SST to analyze the procedures necessary for I/O operations in an 8080-based system. In the following experiment we are concerned only with I/O write operations. Experiment 6 will deal with I/O read events.

When performing an I/O write operation, the microprocessor goes through the following sequence of events:

1. **Address Asserted**. The address bus of the system is set to the address (select code) of the I/O port to which we wish to write. Remember that the address bus is usually under the control of the microprocessor (CPU).

2. **Status Word**. The data bus is set to the status word for an I/O write operation (status word = 0010000). This status information signals the system that an I/O port is about to be written to.

3. **Sync Strobe**. The sync output of the CPU is now set to logical 1 voltage level. This enables the status strobe circuitry to latch the status word for later use.

4. **Sync Off**. To complete the latching of the status word, the sync signal is now set to a logical 0. Any change in the status word is now ignored by the system because the status word latch is disabled when sync is at logical 0.

5. **Data Set**. The data going to the selected I/O port (Step 1) is now placed on the system data bus by the CPU. If the status word had not been latched in Steps 3 and 4, it would now be lost, overridden by the new data just placed on the system data bus.

6. **$\overline{WR}$ Asserted**. To signal the system that all is now ready for an I/O write operation to take place, the $\overline{WR}$ signal from the 8080 now goes to logical 0 (0 state active). The system control signal, which is usually called $\overline{I/OW}$, is now forced by the system to logical 0 (active).

7. **$\overline{WR}$ Off**. The 8080 now resets the $\overline{WR}$ signal to its inactive state of logical 1. The write data on the data bus (Step 5) is now transferred to the selected output port (address still on the address bus).

OBJECTIVES

1.   To identify the system blocks used in an I/O port transfer of data

2.   To understand the signals that are required and their sequence of assertion in an I/O read, and

3.   To examine the address, data and control signals used during an I/O write operation.

INSTRUMENTS AND MATERIALS

1   8080 microprocessor training system

1   Static Stimulus Tester

1   MCS-80 User's Manual

1   Logic Probe

1   Set of system schematics

Recommended Reading: Reference 1
                          Pages 1-6, 8-10, 142-164

PROCEDURE

Step 1

Refer to the schematic of the training system that is under study and identify all input, output and input/output ports in the system. Figure A-6 in the Appendix shows the I/O structure of the Creative Microprocessor System's (CMS) trainer; Note that there is one output port and one input port. The select codes for these ports are determined and set independently by DIP switches IC2 and IC3. The read data is set by DIP switch IC14).

1.1   Make a schematic sketch of each I/O port in your system. Determine the select codes for each port. How can the select codes in your system be changed to a new code?

1.2   The 8080 uses only 8 address lines for I/O select codes. The lower 8 address lines (A7 to A0) carry the same information as the upper 8 address lines (A15 to A8). What is the maximum number of distinct I/O ports possible in an 8080 system? Which address lines are used for I/O select codes in your system?

Step 2

Set up your microprocessor trainer with the SST installed. (Make sure that the 8080 that is removed is stored in conductive foam to avoid damaging it.)

2.1   Set the SST switches into these unasserted positions:

A15 to A0 =	00000000 00000000	(ON)
D7 to D0 =	00000000	(ON)
DBIN =	0	(ON)
$\overline{WR}$ =	1	(OFF)
SYNC =	0	(ON)
8080/8085 =	8080	

Using a logic probe or similar voltage sensing device, verify that the system address bus, data bus, and control bus are now inactive.

Step 3

We now begin the I/O write operation. To check that the procedure is successful, we write the data $AA_{16} = 10101010_2$ to the system display. Refer to the system schematics, and locate the output LEDS, or other display. What is the select code for this output port?

Display Select Code = _____

Note: If your system uses memory mapped I/O for the display,

37

select another port that uses standard I/O so it can be checked with a logic probe.

3.1   Set the address switches on the SST to the following positions:

A7	A6	A5	A4	A3	A2	A1	A0		
1	0	1	0	1	0	1	0	= AA_{16} = Port Select	

Check to verify that the address bus now contains this select code and that the port also has this data at its port select decode circuitry pins.

3.2   Next, we generate and latch the status word for a memory write operation. Set the data switches on the SST (SW3) to the status word for an I/O write (00010000). Verify that the data bus now has this information on it. Check the output of the status word latch used in your system and verify that the status word is not yet equal to 00010000 (unless you have just done an I/O write operation). Set the sync switch on the SST to logical 1 and check the status strobe input to the status latch of your system. If you are using a logic probe it will blink, because the sync signal is normally combined with the Phase 1 clock of the system (See Experiment 9). This check indicates that the status strobe is reaching the status latch.

Finally, set the sync switch on the SST to logical 0 and check that the status word has been held in the status latch. Change the status word set of SW3 of the SST and verify that the status word at the latched output does not change.

3.3   We now place the write data on the system data bus. Set the DIP switch, SW3, on the SST to equal the data AA = 10101010. With a logic probe, verify that the system data bus now contains this data.

3.4   To complete the write operation, the WR signal must be asserted. Set the WR switch on the SST to logical 0. Check that this signal is now present at the I/O select decode circuitry of your system. (It may be inverted, depending on what kind of decoding is performed by the I/O port).

3.5   Set the WR switch on the SST back to logical 1 and observe the system output display. The data AA should now be displayed, signifying completion of the I/O write operation.

Step 4

The microprocessor executes this very same sequence of events each time an output write operation is performed. Change the data written in Step 4 (AA_{16}) to another value and repeat the write procedure. If convenient, change the select code for the display port as set at the port and try to write the original data, AA_{16}, to the port. The select code that is sent to the port must always agree with the hardwired code at the port in order for that particular port to be written to or read from.

Step 5

Repeat Steps 1 through 5 until you have a good feeling for how data is transferred from the microprocessor (SST in this case) to an I/O port in an 8080 based system.

QUESTIONS

1.   What is the status word for an I/O write operation? Could any other values for the status word work on your system?

2.   How many I/O ports can be written to at a time?

3.   What device(s) in the system ensures that write operations will be performed in the prescribed sequence and timed correctly?

4. Draw a schematic of one of the I/O ports in your system and label the control, address, and data busses.

EXPERIMENT 6
READING DATA FROM I/O PORTS

DISCUSSION

In addition to being able to output information, the micro-processor must have some means of reading data coming in from the outside world. As we will see, the sequence of events for an I/O read operation is very similar to an I/O write operation.

The order of events for an input read operation is:

1. Address Asserted. The select code of the I/O port that is to be read is set on the address bus by the micropro-cessor.

2. Status Word. The status word for an I/O port read operation is placed on the system data bus (status word = 0100010).

3. Sync Strobe. The 8080 now sets the sync signal output to logical 1 in order to latch the status word.

4. Sync Off. The sync signal is forced to logical 0 to complete the strobing of the status word.

5. DBIN Set. To this point, the read operation has been the same as the write operation with the exception of the status word (write = 0010000, read = 01000010). Now a new signal is required. The DBIN output of the 8080 tells the system that the 8080 is now ready to receive data. It is the external system's responsibility at this point to put the read data from the selected I/O port on the data bus. To accomplish this, the DBIN signal is forced to logical 1 (active high) and the system generates an I/O signal that tells the selected I/O port to place its data on the system data bus. The CPU now has the

41

input port data present at its data bus pins, where it is then stored in some internal register (usually the accumulator).

7. **DBIN Off.** The microprocessor now resets the DBIN signal to logical 0, thus terminating the data transfer from the selected I/O port.

Notice that time has been ignored in the preceding discussion. By eliminating this restriction one can study the signals generated in the system in a static fashion, taking as long as needed to analyze each step. The use of the static stimulus tester makes this possible.

At the conclusion of Experiment 6, one should have a better comprehension of the electrical events that occur in a microprocessor system as it performs input/output operations.

OBJECTIVES

1. To identify the system blocks used in an I/O port transfer of data

2. To examine the address, data and control signals used during an I/O read operation, and

3. To recall the required signals and their sequence of assertion in an I/O read.

INSTRUMENTS AND MATERIALS

1   8080 microprocessor training system

1   Static Stimulus Tester (SST)

1   MCS-80 User's Manual

1   Logic probe

Recommended reading: Reference 1
                          Pages 142-164

PROCEDURE

Step 1

In an input read operation the first electrical event to occur is the setting of the address of the input port on the system address bus. In standard operation, the address bus of a system is under the control of the CPU, except in this experiment the bus is controlled by the static stimulus tester.

1.1   Install the SST in place of the CPU and set the $\overline{WR}$ switch = 1 position, DBIN switch = 0 position and the SYNC switch = 0 position. (These are the unasserted logic levels for these control signals for an 8080 CPU).

1.2   Find the select code of the port that is to be read. This information should be on your system schematic.

Read port select code =_____ 2

1.3   Set the address switches, A_7-A_0 on the SST (SW1) to the select code found in Step 1.2.

1.4   Using a logic probe, verify that the selected input port now has an active select signal.

Step 2

The next electrical event to occur in the read operation is the latching of the status word. The status word that is latched is the one that corresponds to an input read operation. The latching of the status word occurs from these three operations:

a.   The data bus outputs the status word 42_{16}.

b.   The SYNC signal on the CPU goes to logical 1.

c.   The SYNC signal on the CPU goes to logical 0.

2.1   Now, let us perform these same three events using the Static Stimulus Tester (SST). First, we set the status word

43

for an input operation onto the data bus. This is accomplished by setting the data switches on the SST (SW3) to these positions:

D1=OFF, D6=OFF;   logical 1

D0=D2=D3=D4=D5=D7=ON;   logical 0

This action places the status word 42_{16} on the data bus. The LEDs D1 and D6 on the SST board will be on. All other LEDs on the SST board will be off.

2.2   To latch the status word we set the SYNC switch on the SST to logical 1. Using a logic probe, verify that the SYNC signal is now at logical 1.

2.3   Set the SYNC switch on the SST board to logical 0. This action disables the status strobe signal from the status latches. Verify that the status strobe is no longer enabled to the status latches by placing the logic probe at the appropriate latch pin on your system. The status word is now latched.

Step 3

Set the data at the input port whose select code was chosen in Step 1.2 to AA_{16}. If the data is fixed by the port and cannot be altered, determine what data will be read.

Input Data = _____$_2$

Step 4

To enable the input port data onto the data bus we must set the DBIN switch on the SST board to logical 1. This does two things:

a.   It asserts the $\overline{\text{I/OR}}$ control bus signal, and

b.   It enables the bi-directional data bus buffers (in the correct direction) for the CPU to receive data from the system.

4.1   If you have not done so, set the DBIN switch on
the SST board to logical 1. Now the $\overline{\text{I/OR}}$ control bus signal is
asserted. Check the control bus lines for proper logic levels
at the termination points.

Step 5

The read circuit is now complete. There is an electrical
path from the input port to the data pins on the SST. The
system buffers are enabled (in the correct direction) by the
logical state of the DBIN signal. The bi-directional buffers
can receive data on the data bus and input this data to the data
input pins of the SST.

We can see the data the CPU would read by examining the
LEDs on the SST board. These LEDs correspond to the data that
would appear at the CPU data pins.

5.1   The read data in the SST display is _____ 2
Does this correspond to the expect data (data expected to be
read) noted in Step 3?

Step 6

Set the DBIN switch on the SST to the logical 0 position.
This disables the input port data from the data bus. It also
reverses the direction of the bi-directional data bus buffers.
(The SST now has regained control of the system data bus).

Setting the DBIN signal to logical 0 terminates the data
transfer. Prior to this, the DBIN signal was logical 1, and the
CPU would have strobed the data into an internal register.

Step 7

Keeping in mind the order of electrical events, try to read
data from other I/O ports in your system. Record the I/O select
codes and expect data in Table 6-1.

TABLE 6-1   Input/Output port select codes and
expected data to be read from the ports. Record
in hexadecimal form.

I/O SELECT CODE (HEX)	EXPECT DATA (HEX)

QUESTIONS

1.   With the 8080, is the DBIN signal active high or active low?

2.   Summarize the events that are necessary for an I/O read operation.

3.   What would happen if the 8080 tried to read a write-only port?

4.   List three common types of I/O structures used in microprocessor systems. Draw a schematic that is typical of each configuration.

5.   If an I/O select code of FF_{16} were placed on the system address bus, what would be the value of A_{15}-A_8?

6.   Is $1FE_{16}$ a valid I/O select code for your system? Why or why not?

EXPERIMENT 7
TRANSFERRING DATA BETWEEN I/O AND MEMORY

DISCUSSION

At this point in our experiments we have developed the techniques and understanding of how the system hardware moves data to and from the system RAM memory and the I/O ports. Now we complete the cycle of data flow by examining the transfer of data from RAM memory to an I/O port and back to memory.

When data is moved by the microprocessor from memory to a selected I/O port it is routed normally through one or more registers in the 8080. For data to bypass the microprocessor a technique called Direct Memory Access (DMA) must be used. (We will not investigate DMA at this time because it is very dependent on the system hardware and requires an understanding of interrupts). The primary internal CPU register through which data is passed to I/O ports is the accumulator, or A register. Unless memory-mapped I/O is present in the system, data from memory must go through the accumulator on its way to a selected I/O port. See Figure 7-1.

The SST simulates the 8080 microprocessor in this experiment; however, the SST does not have an internal register for temporary data storage. Therefore, at certain times in the following procedure the experimenter must act as a register and simply record the data bus contents by hand.

The order of events for moving data from an I/O port to memory is:

1. Select the I/O port to be read

2. Enable this port, and record the data now forced onto

47

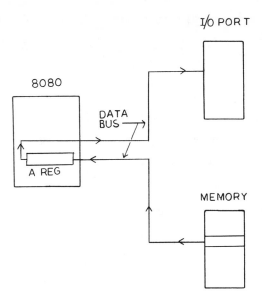

FIGURE 7-1   Flow of data from memory to an I/O port (except for the case of memory mapped I/O)

the system data bus and displayed by the LEDs on the SST

    3.   Address the desired memory location in the RAM portion of the memory, and

    4.   Write the data recorded in Step 2 into the addressed memory location.

    To transfer data from a memory location to a specific I/O port these four procedures are used:

    a.   Address the desired memory location (RAM or ROM)

    b.   Read the location, and record the data returned on the system data bus

    c.   Select the appropriate I/O port where the data is to go, and

    d.   Write the data recorded in Step 2 to the selected port.

    Later we will see how a microprocessor can be instructed to

perform these transfer operations by means of software.

OBJECTIVES

1. To understand the signal paths that data takes in going from memory to I/O and from I/O to memory, and

2. To learn the sequence of events needed to perform data transfers effectively between memory and I/O.

INSTRUMENTS AND MATERIALS

1   8080 microprocessor training system

1   Static Stimulus Tester (SST)

1   MCS-80 User's Manual

1   Logic probe or digital voltmeter

Recommended Reading: Reference 1
                                      Pages 129-164

PROCEDURE

Step 1

First, we will read some known data at a system input port using the SST.

1.1   Remove the 8080 and connect the SST to your system through the system's 8080 socket.

1.2   Set the data at any system I/O port to a known value. Select code =_____ $_{16}$.

1.3   Following the steps outlined in Experiment 6, read the data at the port you have selected. The data should now be on the system data bus and displayed on the LED display of the SST. Record the data, and verify that it agrees with the data set at the port in Step 1.2.

Step 2

Now we write the data recorded in Step 1.3 to a valid RAM
location.

2.1   Following the procedure in Experiment 4 for
writing to memory, write the data recorded in Step 1.3 to a
valid RAM location. The exact location is dictated by the
electrical memory map configuration of your system.

2.2   Change the data at the I/O port selected in
Step 1.2 and repeat Steps 1.3 through 2.1. Check that the
selected memory locations do indeed contain the data at the
selected port.

Step 3

Now we reverse the process and write the data from memory
to an I/O port. The system display is used as the destination
for the data now in memory.

3.1   Using the procedure in Experiment 4, read the
data from memory written in Step 2 above. Check that the data
now in the SST's display agrees with the original data written
in Step 2.

3.2   Determine the select code for the system display.
Write the data obtained in Step 3.1 to the system display using
the procedure outlined in Experiment 5, Step 3.

Note: If your system uses memory-mapped I/O for the display, use the select code as a memory address and perform a
memory write operation as detailed in Experiment 4, Step 2.
Check that the system display now agrees with the SST display.

Step 4

4.1   To gain a good feeling for what is happening in
this data transfer procedure, repeat Steps 1 through 4, using

different I/O ports and data. Using a logic probe or other means of testing the logic level, check to be sure at each step that the address and data buses contain the correct information.

QUESTIONS

1.   If DMA allows data to go directly from an I/O port to memory, what would be an advantage of DMA over data transfer through the 8080?

2.   Through how many internal 8080 registers (maximum) can data be routed in going between memory and I/O?

3.   How many data words are transferred between memory and I/O during each operation?

4.   How is data routed through the 8080 in going from memory to an I/O port?

5.   List possible status words for memory read, memory write, I/O read and I/O write operations. Which bits in each case must be decoded? Assume no other system operations will be performed.

EXPERIMENT 8
SYSTEM POWER REQUIREMENTS

<u>DISCUSSION</u>

How much current will a total system require from its DC power supply (or supplies)? This question arises and must be answered every time an electronics system is designed, added to, or modified in some way. For microprocessors, as for the majority of electronics systems, we need to recall that in the basic organization the DC power supply typically furnishes power to a number of parallel load circuits. This is shown in Figure 8-1. Note that the total source current drawn from the DC power supply is found by adding the currents of all of the parallel branches: $I_S = I_1 + I_2 + I_3$, etc.

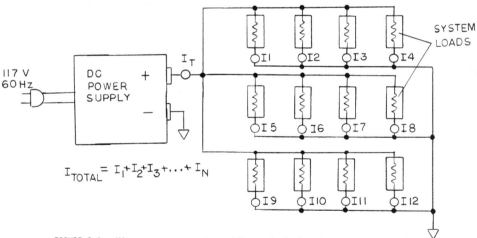

FIGURE 8-1   Microprocessor systems, like most electronic systems, are made-up of a number of parallel load circuits connected to a DC power supply as shown.

A precaution to note is that the current drawn by a particular IC load circuit is different at logical 1 from its current at logical 0. (Device specifications tell maximum, minimum and typical operating currents). So the question of what is required of a DC power supply must be rephrased to ask: What is the typical operating current? Or perhaps: What is the "worst case" current if all loads draw maximum current at the same time? To find this, all of the parallel elements that make up the total load on a power supply must be identified, their typical or worst case operating currents determined, and these added together to find I_S. The DC power supply must be capable of holding its specified output voltage under the highest current load conditions.

Each time another parallel branch is added, more current must be supplied by the DC power supply. At some point, any further increase in load current will exceed the capacity of the power supply. Then, the voltage drop which that load current creates across the source resistance will increase, and the output voltage to the load will fall below its specified value. Excessive load on a power supply can occur as a result of adding too many load elements, a defective IC that draws too much current, a short between PC board traces (which represents another parallel current path), or inadvertently overloading a power supply by miscalculating how much current the load requires.

What we have said about loads on the DC power supply has significance for loads connected to any kind of voltage source. For example, each IC that handles the various logical signals can be thought of as a voltage source with its load consisting of the ICs connected to its output. Too many load elements (or a short) causes the logical output voltage of the IC to fall, sometimes outside the boundary of a logical 1 or logical 0, because the drive capability limit of the voltage source has been exceeded. One of the basic reasons for using buffers is to increase the drive capability of a bus line where the load requirements exceed the current capability of the original signal source. Refer to Experiment 3 and note the use of address buffers where the drive capability of the microprocessor signal source is not large enough to handle all of the parallel elements of the imposed load.

Now in Experiment 8, we carry on our investigation of the organization of microprocessor circuits begun in Experiment 3, which focused on the 3-bus architecture that is typical of these systems. This time, we look at the details of how parallel loads relate to a voltage source: first at the DC power supply for the microprocessor system, and then at the signal sources and the loads they drive within the system.

OBJECTIVES

1.   To examine the organization of a microprocessor system in relation to its DC power supply

2.   To learn how to determine the total load that a microprocessor system imposes on its DC power supply

3.   To calculate the total current requirements of the particular microprocessor system used in this experiment, and

4.   To examine the use of buffers as a solution to an overloaded signal or signal line.

INSTRUMENTS AND MATERIALS

1   8080 microprocessor training system

1   TTL Data Book

1   MCS-80 User's Manual

54

Recommended Reading: Reference 1
                         Pages 11, 12, 112, 113

PROCEDURE

Step 1

1.1   Refer to the schematic diagram of your system and carefully compare its organization with that shown in Figure 8-1. Does your system consist of a number of parallel load circuits as Figure 8-1 suggests?

1.2   Make a table similar to Table 8-1, listing all ICs in your microprocessor system. (You may recall that you already made such a list in Experiment 1; refer to it, and, if you are satisfied that it is complete, you may draw from it in setting up Table 8-1.) Look up the specifications of each device listed and complete the table by filling in the current

TABLE 8-1 System Integrated Circuit parameters. NOTE: VREQ = voltage required of the DC power supply for the indicated device and REQUIV = equivalent resistance of the device; REQUIV = VREQ/Typical operating current

DEVICE TYPE	TYPICAL OPERATING CURRENT	MAXIMUM CURRENT (MA)	V_{REQ} (VOLTS)	R_{EQUIV} (KOHMS)	DEVICE FUNCTION IN THE SYSTEM

and voltage values.

1.3　　　　When all devices have been listed and Table 8-1 is complete, calculate the total load current (I_T) drawn from the DC power supply, based on the typical operating current of each device listed.

1.4　　　　Calculate the equivalent resistance of the total system load on the power supply:

$$R_{eq} = \frac{V_S}{I_T}$$

1.5　　　　If the specifications of your system give power supply current, compare this specified value with your calculated figure for I_T. Examine your system carefully, and if it is convenient and easy to do so, measure I_T and compare the measured value with the value calculated in Step 1.3. What do you find?

Step 2

2.1　　　　Look carefully at the number of parallel load elements that connect to each address line. (See your system schematic and refer to Experiment 3 3-bus architecture). Now, look up the current drive capability of the 8080A microprocessor. This is found in the 8080A specifications. Note this number, and compare it with the input drive required by the address line buffer (if one is present in your system).

2.2　　　　Next, look up the input drive current required by each of the parallel loads connected to the address lines. Add these values to find the total load current that each address line must supply. Compare this total with the output drive capability of the buffer, and then with the output drive capability of the microprocessor. What do you find?

56

QUESTIONS

1. On the basis of your data, would you conclude that the DC power supply of your system is lightly loaded, has some reserve capacity, or is at maximum load? Explain.

2. If additional circuitry is to be added to the system, such as an another I/O port or additional memory, would the present power supply be adequate? How, exactly, would you check to find out?

3. What will be the most likely result if the system is modified and the change causes the load to exceed the rating of the power supply?

4. If the output signal drive of a microprocessor or other device is insufficient to meet the requirements of its load, how can this problem be resolved?

5. How many examples can you find in your microprocessor system where buffers are used to solve the problem of the load being greater than the signal source can supply?

6. What will be the likely result if the output signal drive capability of a device is exceed because the inputs of too many load devices are connected to it?

7. What are the differences in input loading between MOS, TTL (low power) and TTL (Schottky) logic families? Be specific.

EXPERIMENT 9
SYSTEM CLOCKS

<u>DISCUSSION</u>

Most microprocessor systems are synchronous in nature. For a system or device to be sychronous, its actions must be in step with one or more clocks that may be internal or external to the system. This means that the execution of an instruction by a microprocessor is done at a rate determined by the system clock(s). The nature and specification of the clocks for an 8080 system are the subject of this experiment.

For the 8080 to function at all, two free-running clock signals must be generated and input to the device. These signals have the same peak-to-peak amplitude and frequency, but are out of phase with each other. The phase relationship between the two clocks is defined precisely by the manufacturer. Figure 9-1 shows the relative shape and phasing of the 8080 clock signals, which are called Phase 1 (ϕ_1) and Phase 2 (ϕ_2). Note that there are four non-overlapping transitions when the timing of the two phases is considered and compared. By providing two leading and two trailing edges, Phases 1 and 2 give the 8080 four distinct times with which to clock its internal circuitry. This is the reason for using the two-phase clocks.

Unlike the other input signals to the 8080, Phases 1 and 2 are required to be at MOS logic voltage levels, approximately 0 volts = logical 0, +12 volts = logical 1. This means that standard active pull-up TTL devices cannot be used to drive the clock inputs of the 8080 (Pins 15 and 22) directly. When clock signals of appropriate phase and frequency are generated with

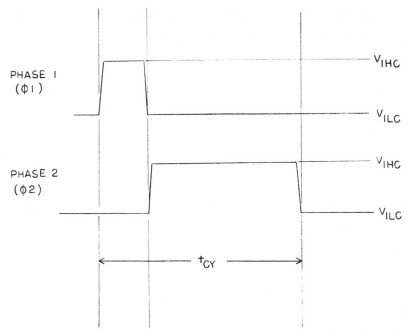

FIGURE 9-1   Relationship of VIHC, VILC and t_{CY} parameters to the waveforms of Phase 1 and Phase 2

TTL, the signals must be level shifted to 12V. Additionally, the rise and fall time of the generated clock signals must be closely considered. If the transition times from a logical 1 level to a logical 0 level (or vice versa) are too slow, reliable operation of the 8080 is not guaranteed by the manufacturer. The dynamic nature of the 8080's internal MOS circuitry requires that the transition times meet certain specifications.

Besides requirements relating to the edge transition times, the frequency of the Phase 1 and Phase 2 clocks must be within prescribed limits. If the clocks are too slow, the dynamic MOS circuitry of the 8080 will stop functioning correctly. Similarly, if the clocks are set too fast the internal circuits of the 8080 will not be able to keep up with the pace. We will see what the exact limits on frequency, amplitude, and phasing are for the 8080 clocks during this experiment.

OBJECTIVES

1.   To become familiar with the system clocks for an 8080 based system

2.   To verify the manufacturer's specifications of clock requirements, and

3.   To demonstrate a possible circuit for generating Phase 1 and Phase 2 signals required by the 8080.

INSTRUMENTS AND MATERIALS

1   8080 microprocessor training system

1   TTL data book

1   MCS-80 User's Manual

1   Oscilloscope (dual channel with a bandwidth greater
    than 10 MHZ) An oscilloscope with less bandwidth
    may be used but exact measurements might be difficult
    to make.

Recommended Reading: Reference 1
                           Pages 113-124, 234-239

PROCEDURE

Step 1

First, we examine the manufacturer's data sheets and determine the requirements for Phase 1 and 2.

1.1   Referring to the 8080 User's Manual, find the clock input low voltage (VILC) and clock input high voltage (VIHC) specifications under DC characteristics for the 8080. Record the minimum and maximum values in Table 9-1A. If the DC power supply (V_{DD}) is set to 12.0 volts, what are the limits on VIHC?

Minimum VIHC = _____

Maximum VIHC = _____

TABLE 9-1   Phase 1 and Phase 2 clock parameters
(from MCS-80 User's Manual)

CLOCK LEVEL	MIN (VOLTS)	MAX (VOLTS)
V_{ILC}		
V_{IHC}		

CYCLE TIME	MIN (NSEC)	MAX (NSEC)
t_{CY}		

(A)   (B)

If the V_{SS} power supply is at 0 volts can the clocks swing below ground? If so, by how many volts?

1.2   Now, find the clock period specification (t_{cy}) under the 8080 AC characteristics in the User's Manual. Recall that period is defined as the time of one cycle, in seconds, when frequency is measured in Hertz. Enter in Table 9-1B. If the period of an AC signal is known, its corresponding frequency can be determined by the formula:

Frequency = 1/Period

Calculate the minimum and maximum operating frequency for the 8080 and enter the value in Table 9-2. Complete the rest of Table 9-2 for the 8080A-1 and the 8080A-2. Note the differences in the operating speeds; these differences are good reasons for selecting one version of an 8080 over another. One should also consider that higher speed versions are usually more expensive.

1.3   Referring to the MSC-80 User's Manual, find the clock specifications for rise and fall time (t_r, t_f). If the

61

DEVICE	OPERATING FREQUENCY	
	MIN (MHZ)	MAX
8080A		
8080A-1		
8080A-2		
M8080A		

Phase 1 clock has a rise time of 75nSec, is the 8080A guaranteed
to function properly? Are there any differences between the
8080A, 8080A-1 and 8080A-2 clock transition times? Make a
sketch of the Phase 1 signal, using the minimum specifications
given for the 8080A, and label t_r and t_f.

1.4   Complete Table 9-3A for the 8080A. Refer to
Figure 9-2 for the physical meaning of the specifications of
Table 9-3. The duty cycle of a digital signal is calculated by:

$$\text{Duty Cycle} = \frac{\text{Time Logical 1}}{(\text{Time Logical 1} + \text{Time Logical 0})}$$

TABLE 9-3 (A) 8080A clock transition times (expressed in nSEC)
(B) Calculated duty cycles for the 8080A clocks (no units)

	RISE AND FALL TIMES	MIN (NSEC)	MAX (NSEC)
(A)	PHASE 1		
	PHASE 2		

	DUTY CYCLE	MIN	MAX
(B)	PHASE 1		
	PHASE 2		

Calculate the minimum and maximum duty cycles for Phase 1 and 2
based on the clock specifications given for the 8080A. Record in
Table 9-3B.

Step 2

Now that we have determined what the requirements are for
the Phase 1 and Phase 2 clocks, let us examine the signals as
they exist in an actual system.

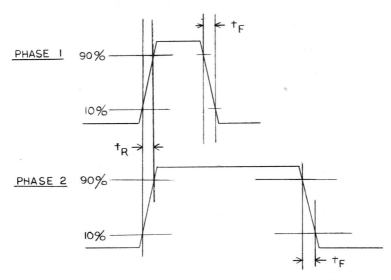

FIGURE 9-2 Relationship of Rise (tr) and Fall(tf) Time specifications to 8080 clock waveforms. Note: 10% = 10% of the total voltage swing.

2.1   Apply power to your microprocessor system and check which version of the 8080 is installed as the CPU. What should be the minimum and maximum operating frequency for this system? (See specifications of t_{cy} and calculate as in Step 1.2).

2.2   Connect an oscilloscope to the 8080 as follows:

Channel 1 (A) to Pin 22 of the 8080 (Phase 1)

Channel 2 (B) to Pin 15 of the 8080 (Phase 2)

Place the oscilloscope in the alternate mode at a sweep rate of 0.5 uSec per division. Set the input attenuation in both channels for 2 volts per division (including any probe attenuation). Trigger the oscilloscope on Channel 1 (A). You should now have a display similar to Figure 9-1. Make sure that the probes are properly grounded through a ground strap at the probe end of the cable. Measure and record the parameters as indicated in Table 9-4.

2.3   Compare the results of Step 2.2 against those of Step 1 for your particular 8080 version. How much overshoot and undershoot do Phase 1 and 2 have, as observed on the oscilli-scope? Based on the specifications of Step 1, what are the limits on these two parameters? Are the results obtained from measurement within the limits of the specification?

TABLE 9-4   Measured clock parameters for the 8080 system clocks. Indicate the grade of the 8080 used in your system

t_R (NSEC)	t_F (NSEC)	FREQUENCY (MHZ)	DUTY CYCLE	COMMENTS
NOTES				

Step 3

We now examine the circuitry that generates the clocks for the 8080. Remember, some microprocessors do not need an external clock source, but generate their clock signals internally as does the 8085.

3.1   Review the schematic for your system. Redraw the portion that shows the clock generators. Figure 9-3 shows how the clocks of the CMS trainer are generated. Is the frequency of your system clocks crystal controlled? Why is this a good idea in a 8080-based system? If the phasing or amplitude of your clock circuit can be varied, change Phases 1 and 2 to 100 KHZ. Does the 8080 operate at this frequency? If possible,

lower the clock voltage levels to +5 volts, logical 1, and check
the system operation.

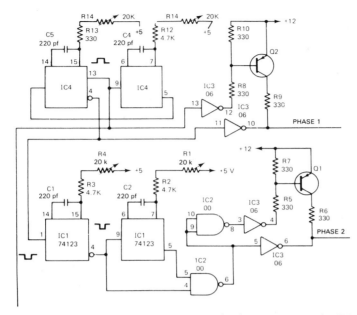

FIGURE 9-3 Creative Microprocessor Systems (CMS) training system's 8080
clock generator schematic

Step 4

A commonly used large-scale integrated (LSI) device that is
used to generate the ϕ_1 and ϕ_2 clocks for the 8080 is the 8224,
originally developed by Intel Corporation. If your system does
not contain this device, Experiment 9 is complete. If your
system does contain an 8224, proceed as follows:

4.1   With power applied to the system, check the
following pins with an osilloscope on the 8224:

Pin 12	Oscillator output
Pin 11	Phase 1
Pin 10	Phase 2
Pin 6	Phase 2 (TTL level)

Record your results in Table 9-5.

TABLE 9-5   Measured 8224 clock parameters

SIGNAL	t_R (NSEC)	t_F (NSEC)	FREQUENCY (MHZ)	DUTY CYCLE	COMMENTS
OSCILLATOR (OUTPUT)					
PHASE 1					
PHASE 2					
PHASE 2 (TTL LEVEL)					

NOTES

4.2   Verify that the OSC OUT (Pin 12) is nine times the frequency of ϕ_1 and ϕ_2. Refer to MCS-80 User's Manual, Page 6-21.

QUESTIONS

1.   How many oscillators are required (minimum) to generate the clocks for an 8080-based system?

2.   If an 8080A-1 requires 4 t_{cy}s to execute a particular instruction, how much time is required to execute 10 such instructions? Assume the 8080A-1 is operating at maximum speed.

3.   What is the highest frequency of operation of the 8080 family of devices? Express your answer in MHz.

4.   If Phase 1 were measured to be 8.1 volts peak-to-peak in amplitude, would the 8080 system be operational? Assume an

8080A CPU.

5. If your system uses an 8224 clock generator, what minimum frequency is needed to guarantee operation of the 8080A-1?

6. What is the maximum crystal frequency for the device in Question 5?

EXPERIMENT 10
RESETTING THE MICROPROCESSOR

DISCUSSION

Whenever a microprocessor system is turned on, it is important to establish a definite, known starting point for future system operations. We say we "initialize" the system, that is, we use the reset function to place essential portions of the 8080-based system at the designated starting point. Understanding the mechanism for resetting the 8080, and its subsequent effect, is the goal of this experiment.

When power is first applied to an 8080 microprocessor, the state of internal registers, flip-flops and similar devices is unknown. This is true of most microprocessors. Hence, some means of establishing a known state for the system to start at must either be provided externally or performed internally. In the case of the 8080, Pin 12 is designated as a reset input. This pin is normally at logical 0 during operation. When Pin 12 is forced to a logical 1 a series of events takes place that initialize the microprocessor. To summarize:

1.   The contents of the program counter (PC) are set to address 0000_{16}. Because the program counter always contains the next address in memory to be executed, the 8080 begins execution at address 0000_{16} when the reset pin is forced low again at some time in the future.

2.   The interrupt enable (INTE) and hold acknowledge (HLDA) internal flip-flops are both reset to logical 0. The function of these internal devices will not be discussed here, but it is important to remember that they are initialized to a

logical 0 when a reset is performed.

3.   The remaining registers and flags that are accessible to the user through software in the 8080 are not altered. This means that their state is unknown after a reset signal is processed and must be initialized by the system software. For this reason, the first portion of system memory is usually devoted to software instructions that set the 8080 registers to a known state before any more software is executed.

OBJECTIVE

1.   To examine the use and function of the reset input of the 8080, and

2.   To understand the software implications of the reset procedure of the 8080.

INSTRUMENTS AND MATERIALS

1   8080 microprocessor training system

1   MCS-80 User's Manual

1   Digital voltmeter or VOM

1   4.7K 10% 1/4 watt carbon resistor

1   1K 10% 1/4 watt carbon resistor

Recommended Reading: Reference 1
                            Pages 238-239

PROCEDURE

Step 1

In this step, we examine the status of the 8080 when a reset signal is applied.

1.1   Apply power to the 8080 system. Using a digital voltmeter or VOM, measure the voltage on Pin 12 of the 8080. Is the system now in the reset or operation mode?

1.2   Through a 1KOHM resistor, connect the reset pin to 5V. Measure the voltage on Pin 12 again. If it is not now at approximately 5V, turn off the power and remove the 8080 from its socket. Make sure that you are well grounded first. Now, bend Pin 12 out and away from the other pins, then reinsert the 8080 in its socket. Turn the power on again and reconnect Pin 12 to the 5 volt supply through a 1KOHM resistor. The 8080 is now in the reset mode.

1.3   With your voltmeter, check the voltage levels on the address and data pins. Record these in Table 10-1. Now, turn the power off and on and repeat your measurements. Record in Table 10-1. How do the results compare? Explain any differences.

TABLE 10-1   Address and data bus states before and after a system power-on cycle
NOTE: LOGIC EQU = equivalent logic level; 1 or 0

BIT NUMBER	ADDRESS (INITIAL)		DATA (INITIAL)		ADDRESS (FINAL)		DATA (FINAL)		COMMENTS
	VOLT LEVEL	LOGIC EQU	VOLT LEVEL	LOGIC EQU	VOLT LEVEL	LOGIC EQU	VOLT LEVEL	LOGIC EQU	
0									
1									
2									
3									
4									
5									
6									
7									
8									
9									
10									
11									
12									
13									
14									
15									

<u>Step 2</u>

To reset the 8080 whenever power is turned off and on again, a power-on reset circuit can be devised. We will now investigate how this circuit functions.

2.1   Study the circuit in Figure 10-1. What is the voltage at Pin 12 of the 8080 when power is first applied?

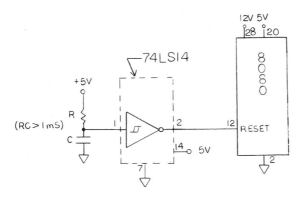

FIGURE 10-1   Example of a power-on reset circuit

2.2   If your system has an 8224, examine Pins 1 and 2 when the system reset is pushed. Do your observations agree with the 8224 block diagram on Page 6-26 in the MCS-80 User's Manual?

<u>Step 3</u>

By attaching a resistor to a tri-state output and measuring the voltage before and after, it can be determined whether the output is in a tri-state mode.

3.1   Put the 8080 in a reset state.

3.2   Check and record in Table 10-2 the voltage levels on all the address, data and control lines (except reset) of the 8080.

3.3   One-by-one check the pins again with a 4.7KOHM resistor connected between the pin and ground or VCC (+5V).

TABLE 10-2   Address, data and control buses during RESET pin being active high;
Logical 1

BIT NUMBER	ADDRESS (INITIAL)		DATA (INITIAL)		CONTROL (CTL) SIGNALS				COMMENTS
	VOLT LEVEL	LOGIC EQU	VOLT LEVEL	LOGIC EQU	VOLT LEVEL	LOGIC EQU	CTL NAME		
0									
1									
2									
3									
4									
5									
6									
7									
8									
9									
10									
11									
12									
13									
14									
15									

Record in Table 10-2. If the logic level on a pin was initially 0 (Step 3.2), then try to pull it to VCC (+5V). Similarly, if the level was 1 try to pull it to ground.

3.4   If the before-and-after levels agree within 0.5 volts, then that pin is tri-stated (has high impedance or is OFF state).

QUESTIONS

1. Which, if any, pins on the 8080 go to a tri-state (OFF) state during reset? Can you think of any advantages to going tri-state during reset?

2. Referring to the MCS-80 User's Manual, how long must the reset pin be high to insure a complete reset has occurred?

3.   Is it a great disadvantage not to clear or set all internal registers during reset? Why or why not?

4.   Which registers are affected by the hardware reset on the 8080?

EXPERIMENT 11
ASSEMBLING AND LOADING A PROGRAM

DISCUSSION

The hardware of any microprocessor system is of little value without proper software to instruct it. Software is the name given to all the written procedures that form the programs used to run a microprocessor system. A program consists of a logical sequence of instructions that the microprocessor can understand and act upon to perform a desired task.

The instructions that make up the programs exist in two basic forms called source code and object code. The most understandable of these (to the program writer) is the source code that is made up of words known as mnemonics. Each mnemonic represents a particular instruction to the microprocessor. The source code consists of a number of mnemonics that are written in a logical order to accomplish some task.

But microprocessors cannot understand letters or words, so the source code must be translated into binary notation which the machine _does_ understand. The conversion from mnemonic code to binary code is called assembling the program. This process of assembling the source code is often performed by a program called an assembler. The assembler program can be written in various computer languages. If the assembler is written for and run on the system where the resulting program will be run, it is called a resident assembler. If the assembler is written in another language (FORTRAN, BASIC, PASCAL, etc.), then it is termed a cross assembler. The result of this conversion is a series of binary numbers that equal the original source code in

74

meaning: that is, each mnemonic contained in the source code corresponds to one, two or three binary words (8 bits per word). The group of all of the binary numbers that emerge from the conversion from the source code is called the object code. Figure 11-1 shows a simple 8080 microprocessor program with each of its equivalent component parts labeled for easy comparison. The program has been assembled, generating corresponding object code.

In addition to the 8080 mnemonics, a source code program contains other mnemonic statements called pseudo instructions that tell the assembler precisely how to translate the 8080 mnemonics. The psuedo instructions are not actually converted into object code but serve to define constants, specify a starting address, name the program, and so forth.

An assembler program is not necessary to form the object code from the source inputs, because the object code can be generated by hand. But this is time-consuming and tedious. However, it is often done for small programs, or when another computer or microprocessor system is not available to run the assembler program. The supplementary instructions required by the assembler (the pseudo instructions) have no meaning to the microprocessor itself, but are used only to control the assembler while it is generating the object code from the mnemonics of the source code. The pseudo instructions are defined by the particular assembler program that is used.

The source code that we will use is also called assembly language. Assembly language is one of the most basic computer languages in that it allows manipulation of information directly in the microprocessor itself. Numerous assembler programs have been written, each with its own set of rules for operation. In this experiment and throughout this laboratory manual, we will deal only with the hand procedures that are necessary for translating a source program into object code. Additionally, we will follow the source code format shown in Figure 11-1 and used in the MCS-80 User's Manual.

The 8080 microprocessor contains internally a number of temporary locations called registers. These registers are locations where information can be manipulated by various instructions that are part of the software for the 8080 microprocessor. Each type of microprocessor has its own set of in-

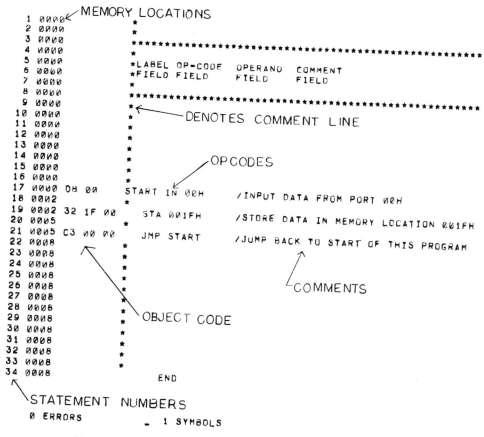

FIGURE 11-1   Source Code format used in this laboratory manual

structions, which are defined by the manufacturer.

Figure 11-2 shows a diagram of all the 8080 registers that are accessible by software. Initially, consider the A register, often called the accumulator. The characteristics that distinguish this register from the others is that certain instructions work only on the 8 bits of data contained in the accumulator. In particular, most of the arithmetic, logical and shifting operations must use the A register during their execution (see Experiments 14 and 15).

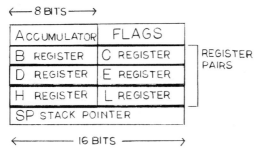

FIGURE 11-2   Internal software registers of the 8080 (user accessable)

This introductory laboratory in software demonstrates the procedure needed to translate (assemble) an object code program from a specific source code, and shows how to load the object code form of the program into memory and then run it.

OBJECTIVES

1.   To learn how microprocessor programs are assembled into object code and loaded into the system memory

2.   To learn how programs can be loaded into different locations in memory and the limitations involved in the process, and

3.   To assemble, load, and run a sample program.

INSTRUMENTS AND MATERIALS

1   8080 microprocessor training system

1   MCS-80 User's Manual

Recommended Reading: Reference 1
                         Pages 168-170, 179

PROCEDURE

Step 1

In this and following steps we examine the use, assembly, and loading of the 8080 instructions shown in Table 11-1.

TABLE 11-1   Initial set of 8080 mnemonics. Refer to Chapter 4 of the MCS-80 User's Manual and study the symbol description on page 4-3

MNEMONIC	NUMBER OF BYTES REQUIRED	OP CODE (HEX)	OPERAND	FUNCTION OF INSTRUCTION
IN	2	DB	PORT ADDR.	1 BYTE OF DATA IS MOVED FROM AN I/O PORT TO THE A REGISTER
OUT				
LDA				
STA				
JMP				
HLT				
NOP				
NOTES				

1.1   Referring to Chapter 4 of the MCS-80 User's Manual, complete Table 11-1. The first entry is shown to get the process started. This small set of instructions allows the programmer to transfer data between the system memory and Input/Output port(s).

<u>Step 2</u>

For any mnemonics to work in a microprocessor, they must first be translated into the corresponding object code and loaded into the system memory. The microprocessor can read and execute only those instructions that are located in memory. In addition, the order and location where the object code is loaded into memory is very important. Figure 11-3 shows how these mnemonics could be grouped in sequence to form a program. The purpose of the program is to:

1.   Input data (1 byte) from an I/O port (select code AA_{16})

2.   Store the data in memory location $00F0_{16}$

3.   Read the data in memory locations $00F1_{16}$

4.   Output the read data to I/O port BB_{16}, and

5.   Jump (JMP) back to the beginning of the program in an endless loop. (In other words, the program never halts).

2.1   Using Table 11-1 as a reference, complete the assembly of the program in Figure 11-3. Note that the initial address for the program is 0000_{16}.

ADDRESS	OBJECT CODE			LABEL	OPCODE	OPERAND	COMMENTS
0000	DB	06		START	IN	AAH	/INPUT DATA TO A REGISTER
0002					STA	00F0H	/STORE THE CONTENTS OF A
0005					LDA	00F1H	/LOAD A REG. FROM 00F1H
0008					OUT	BBH	/OUTPUT TO PORT BB
000A	C3	00	00		JMP	START	/JUMP BACK TO THE BEGINNING
							/OF THE PROGRAM
					END		/TELL THE ASSEMBLER TO STOP.

FIGURE 11-3   8080 Source Code program example (partially assembled)

2.2   Reassemble the program of Step 2 using an initial address of 0100_{16}. What is the starting address for user programs in your system?

FIRST ADDRESS OF USER RAM = _____$-16\cdot$

2.3   Load the program assembled in Step 2.2 (with the correct starting address into your system's RAM. Make sure that you have used correct I/O select codes (the system display could be the output I/O port instead of port BB_{16}).

2.4   Run the program. Can you verify that it is operating correctly?

Step 3

The HLT instruction of the 8080 causes the microprocessor to stop all program execution until reset or a hardware interrupt occurs.

3.1 Replace the JMP instruction in Step 2 with a HLT instruction. Assemble, load, and run the program. How can you verify that the program has run successfully? Try your answer.

Step 4

By making the first instruction in executable user RAM a JMP instruction, a program can be loaded and run at any location in available RAM.

4.1   Reassemble your program of Step 3 so that it can be loaded in the middle of the system's user RAM area.

4.2   Load a JMP instruction at the first locations in the user area of memory. (JMP instruction requires 3 bytes of memory). Jump to the first location in memory where the first instruction of Step 4.1's program could be loaded.

4.3   After loading the program of Step 4.1, run and verify that it has executed.

QUESTIONS

1.   What locations in your system's memory are available

for user programs (RAM)? At what addresses is ROM located?

2.   How can a program in an infinite loop be stopped?

3.   What is the maximum number of bytes necessary to load an 8080 instruction? Minimum number?

4.   How many bytes are needed for any 8080 OP-CODE?

5.   Is it necessary to load a program in sequential memory locations? Why or why not?

6.   What determines if data in memory is interpreted as an OP-CODE, address or data by the 8080?

EXPERIMENT 12
WRITING A PROGRAM

<u>DISCUSSION</u>

The programs, or software, that are written for a microprocessor system are constructed with a specific purpose in mind.
The object is to solve a stated problem through the logical
execution of a series of instructions that comprise the program.
In previous experiments, we started with an existing program and
showed what steps were necessary to execute that program in a
microprocessor system. In this exercise, we start at the con-
ception of a program and investigate each step that must be
taken to formulate a program to solve a stated problem.

The flow chart is the most important tool in organizing a
program into a logical flow of problem solving events. As the
name implies, a flow chart is a graphical representation of a
sequence of instructions that is to take place when a program is
run or executed by a microprocessor. Stated another way, the
flow chart is simply a map of all the conditions and actions
that should occur in a particular program. All possible combinations of events or instructions should be specified in the flow
chart.

Figure 12-1 shows a flow chart that has been constructed
for the indicated program. Table 12-1 lists the most commonly
used flow chart symbols and defines them.

When programs are written to solve rather simple software
problems, the flow chart is often omitted and the source code is
written directly from the problem definition. This practice is
dangerous, however, and in complex operations a flow chart becomes a necessity.

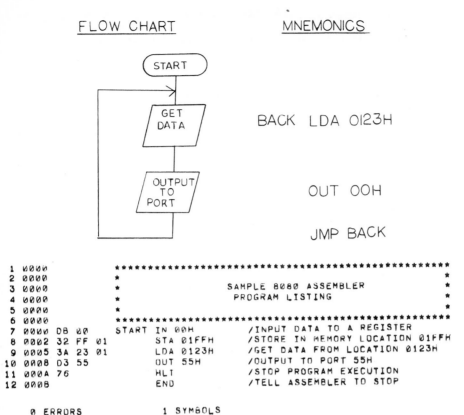

FLOW CHART   MNEMONICS

START

GET
DATA   BACK LDA 0123H

OUTPUT
TO   OUT 00H
PORT

                              JMP BACK

```
 1  0000        ********************************************************
 2  0000        *                                                      *
 3  0000        *           SAMPLE 8080 ASSEMBLER                       *
 4  0000        *           PROGRAM LISTING                             *
 5  0000        *                                                      *
 6  0000        ********************************************************
 7  0000 DB 00  START  IN 00H       /INPUT DATA TO A REGISTER
 8  0002 32 FF 01      STA 01FFH    /STORE IN MEMORY LOCATION 01FFH
 9  0005 3A 23 01      LDA 0123H    /GET DATA FROM LOCATION 0123H
10  0008 D3 55         OUT 55H      /OUTPUT TO PORT 55H
11  000A 76            HLT          /STOP PROGRAM EXECUTION
12  000B               END          /TELL ASSEMBLER TO STOP

    0 ERRORS              1 SYMBOLS
```

FIGURE 12-1 (A) and (B) Representative flow chart and corresponding program

The formulation of a program to solve a specific problem is generally approached in five sequential steps. These are:

1. Define the problem to be solved in words

2. Determine the order of events in the program by drawing a flow chart for solving the problem in question

3. From the flow chart, write out the precise mnemonics of the program

4. Assemble the object code either by hand or with the aid of an assembler program (a working system is required), and

5. Ensure that the program runs, and correct every error found through the use of debugging techniques.

TABLE 12-1   Commonly used flow chart symbols and their meaning

SYMBOL	DESCRIPTION
	TERMINAL SYMBOL - Indicates where the program will start and stop.
	PROCESS SYMBOL - Indicates an operation or calculation will be performed.
	INPUT/OUTPUT SYMBOL - Whenever data is input into the microprocesssor or output to an I/O port this symbol is used.
	DECISION SYMBOL - Indicates a possible transfer or branch in the program based on the condition(s) specified.
	CONNECTION SYMBOL - Indicates connection between signal paths.
	NEXT CHART SYMBOL - Indicates that the flow chart is continued in another location.

If these steps are followed, the problem of program writing becomes a simple step-by-step process.

One addition should be noted -- at each step in program writing, the programmer should include comments as to what the operation or instruction is intended to accomplish. This applies especially to the source code written from a flow chart. Commenting on each line of the program ensures that future users of the program (yourself included) will easily understand the exact operation of your program.

OBJECTIVES

1.   To develop a precise plan or method by which microprocessor programs can be written, and

2.   To write a program that will solve a stated problem.

INSTRUMENTS AND MATERIALS

1   8080 microprocessor training system

1   MCS-80 User's Manual

Recommended Reading: Reference 1
                           Pages 166-173

PROCEDURE

Step 1

Now, we are going to draw a flow chart for a given software problem. We shall construct different flow charts for the same problem, because there are usually several ways to solve a problem, not just one.

1.1   The problem that we are to solve can be stated as:

Move the data from an input I/O port with a known select code to the A register (accumulator) in the 8080. Load this data into memory locations 0023_{16}, 0047_{16}, and $005C_{16}$. Next, read these memory locations sequentially and write the data to a system output port after the read operation. Finally, jump back to the beginning of the program to repeat these operations continually.

One possible solution to this problem is shown in Figure 12-2. Review this example and then draw a second flow chart for the same problem.

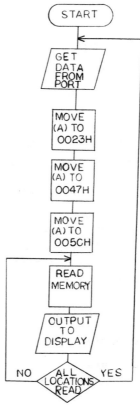

FIGURE 12-2   Sample flow chart for the program example outlined in the procedure

Step 2

Now that two flow charts have been devised for the problem, review the instruction set for the 8080 to find the commands needed to implement the flow chart. Table 12-2 contains a partial listing of instructions that could be used in this program.

TABLE 12-2 MOVE instruction mnemonics for the 8080. See Chapter 4 of the MCS-80
User's Manual

MNEMONIC	NUMBER OF BYTES	OP CODE (HEX)	OPERAND	FUNCTION OF INSTRUCTION	
MOV	1	7E	A,M	M→A	MOVE DATA FROM MEMORY ADDRESS,M,TO A REGISTER
MOV			A,A		
MOV			B,A		
MVI			r,DATA		
MVI			A,DATA		
MOV			M,A		
MOV			C,D		
MOV			H,E		
MOV			L,B		
MOV			E,A		
MOV			L,H		
MOV			H,B		
MOV			C,D		
MOV			A,L		
MOV			D,A		

2.1   Find the origin of the instructions listed in Table 12-2 in the MCS-80 User's Manual and complete Table 12-2 by filling in the function, number of bytes required for the instruction, and Op-Codes that were left blank in the table.

2.2   One possible program realization of the flow chart is shown in Figure 12-3. Assemble this program and load it into the system memory (begin at address 0000H if the CMS trainer is used). Where are programs loaded in your system? Make sure that the I/O select codes are set for the ports in your system. Now, run the program. How can you be sure that the program is executing correctly?

Step 3

3.1   Review the mnemonic instructions in Table 12-2

```
 1 0000          ***********************************************************
 2 0000          *                                                         *
 3 0000          *           SOLUTION PROGRAM                              *
 4 0000          *                                                         *
 5 0000          ***********************************************************
 6 0000 DB 0F    START IN 0FH           /GET DATA FROM PORT 0FH
 7 0002 32 23 00       STA 0023H        /STORE IN MEMORY LOCATION 0023H
 8 0005 32 47 00       STA 0047H        /STORE IN MEMORY LOCATION 0047H
 9 0008 32 5C 00       STA 005CH        /STORE IN MEMORY LOCATION 005CH
10 000B 3A 17 00       LDA 0023         /READ LOCATION 0023H
11 000E D3 00          OUT 00H          /OUTPUT TO PORT 00H
12 0010 3A 47 00       LDA 0047H        /READ LOCATION 0047H
13 0013 D3 00          OUT 00H          /OUTPUT TO PORT 00H
14 0015 3A 5C 00       LDA 005CH        /READ LOCATION 005CH
15 0018 D3 00          OUT 00H          /OUTPUT TO PORT 00H
16 001A                END
```

0 ERRORS   1 SYMBOLS

FIGURE 12-3   Assembler listing of a solution to the flow chart of FIGURE 12-2

again. Without using the LDA or STA instructions, rewrite the program of Step 2. Assemble and load this second version into the system memory. Run the program and verify that it performs correctly.

Step 4

4.1   Change the program of Step 2 so that the three memory locations are each written with different data. For example, write the data 20_{16}, 21_{16}, and 22_{16} into memory locations 23_{16}, 47_{16}, and 50_{16}.

4.2   Assemble, load, and run your program. Check the results.

QUESTIONS

1. Of the programs written in Steps 2 and 3, which is more efficient: that is, which uses the least amount of memory?

2. How can the memory storage locations used in Steps 2 and 3 be read to determine that they have been written into by the program?

3.   Can your programs be loaded at any location in RAM memory?

4.   Why are flow charts necessary in writing programs?

5.   List the steps necessary to write and run a program on any microprocessor system.

REGISTER MANIPULATIONS

DISCUSSION

In this experiment we examine the instructions that allow data to be moved about internally in the 8080 microprocessor. These instructions are important because they are so widely applicable. Although the software we write now may not seem useful, the exercise serves to develop the basic skills and data manipulation techniques that we can use later in larger, more meaningful programs.

Precise techniques for solving a particular software problem are often termed algorithms. For example, a set of instructions that finds the smallest number among, say, 100 random numbers would be called an algorithm. In this experiment and following ones, we will develop various algorithms for solving software problems.

In addition to the A register (accumulator), the 8080 contains six other 8-bit registers that can be accessed through software. These are shown in Figure 11-2, along with the stack pointer, which is a 16-bit register.

Another 16 bit register, the program counter (denoted PC in the literature), is devoted to keeping track of the next address in memory which the microprocessor is to execute. When the 8080 is reset, the PC is automatically reset to 0000_{16}. This means that program execution for the 8080 always begins at address 0000_{16}. At the beginning of execution of each instruction fetched from memory, the program counter is automatically incremented by 1 so it points to the next memory address that the

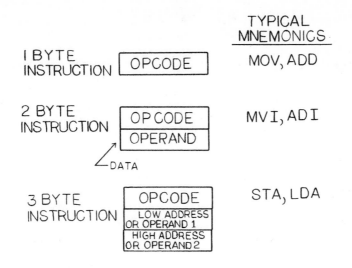

FIGURE 13-1   8080 instruction formats as the Object Code appears in memory

8080 will process. Because the instructions of the 8080 microprocessor are one, two, or three bytes long, the next memory
location is interpreted either as data, a lower address byte, or
another instruction, depending on what kind of instruction is
currently being executed. Figure 13-1 shows this. If the object code is loaded manually, it is the programmer's responsibility to ensure that the program's code is in the correct
sequence. For instance, in a two-byte instruction like ADI, the
second byte must be data, not an address byte or another instruction. Failing to follow proper sequence means trouble and
may cause the program to terminate abnormally.

OBJECTIVES

1.   To become familiar with the supplementary registers
contained in the 8080, and

2.   To develop techniques (algorithms) for transferring
data between the internal registers of the 8080, and between the

internal registers and the outside world.

<u>INSTRUMENTS AND MATERIALS</u>

1   8080 microprocessor training system

1   MCS-80 User's Manual

Recommended Reading: Reference 1
                            Pages 166-170

<u>PROCEDURE</u>

<u>Step 1</u>

The instructions for this exercise are shown in Table 13-1.
Complete Table 13-1 by finding the additional mnemonic instructions in the MCS-80 User's Manual. Remember, there is usually
more than one way to accomplish a given task in software.

TABLE 13-1   A sampling of register manipulation instructions for the 8080. See
Chapter 4 of the MCS-80 User's Manual

MNEMONIC	NUMBER OF BYTES	OP CODE (HEX)	OPERAND	FUNCTION OF INSTRUCTION
MOV	1	NUMEROUS	r2,r1	MOVE DATA FROM REGISTER r1 TO REGISTER r2.
MOV			M,r	
MVI			B,DATA	
LXI				
LDAX				
LHLD				
STAX				
SHLD				
XCHG				

DOUBLE REGISTER INSTRUCTIONS (rows LDAX through XCHG)

NOTES:

Step 2

Draw a flow chart (See Experiment 12 for a discussion of flow charts) to solve the following problem:

2.1   Data from an input port with select code 36_{16} is to be read and stored in the B, C, D, E, H, and L registers. Next, the contents of the B and C registers is to be stored in memory locations 100_8 and 101_8, respectively. Finally, reread the data in memory locations 100_8 and 101_8 and write it to output port 34_{16}. (The contents of memory location 100_8).

If your system does not have selectable I/O port addresses, write the data to the system display and read it from a port with a known address.

2.2   Now, write an 8080 source program that accomplishes the flow chart of Step 1. Assemble and load the program into the trainer and run it. How can you check that your program is operating as expected?

Step 3

Since registers are often used to store data temporarily during program execution, numerous inter-register exchanges are often required. Draw a flow chart to plan the following operation.

3.1   Load Register B with data $D0_{16}$ and Register C with data $3A_{16}$. Then, exchange the contents of the B and C registers with whatever data is currently in the H and L registers. Write the data that is now in memory location 0033_{16} to memory location $003A_{16}$.

Step 4

Using different mnemonics, write two programs in 8080 assembly language that will implement the flow chart of Step 3.

Assemble and load program 1, run it, and verify the results. Do the same with program 2.

Step 5

As time permits, draw a flow chart, write the source code, assemble and run a program that will pass the data AA_{16} from one 8080 register to the next in alphabetical order. In other words, $(A) \rightarrow (B) \rightarrow (C)$ . . . in a continuous loop. How can you check that the program is correctly working?

QUESTIONS

1.   Which program in Step 4 is more efficient in terms of the number of memory locations required for loading the programs? In terms of speed of execution?

2.   How many 16-bit registers in the 8080 are accessible by the programmer?

3.   Why is it more efficient to store temporary data in registers rather than in memory? What would be one disadvantage of temporary register storage?

4.   List all the register pairs in the 8080 and indicate the upper and lower bytes of each pair.

5.   Referring to the MCS-80 User's Manual, list three registers that are not accessible to the programmer.

6.   What are the differences and similarities between an internal 8080 register and a location in memory?

EXPERIMENT 14
ARITHMETIC OPERATIONS

DISCUSSION

After data has been loaded into the microprocessor's internal registers, various kinds of processing may take place. One important category is the combination of the data contained in internal registers through arithmetic. Examples of arithmetic operations that are possible with an 8080 microprocessor are shown in Figure 14-1. Note that the ability to multiply and

ARITHMETIC OPERATION	APPLICABLE 8080 INSTRUCTIONS
ADD (+)	ADD r ADD M ADI DATA ADC r ADC M ACI DATA
SUBTRACT (−)	SUB r SUB M SUI DATA SBB r SBB M SBI DATA

FIGURE 14-1   Arithmetic operations performed by the 8080. See pages 4-6 to 4-7 in the MCS-80 User's Manual.

divide are not included. To perform these functions a series of instructions is necessary. The add and subtract with carry instructions are necessary for doing multibyte arithmetic (double precision). In this experiment, we introduce and use the addition (ADD) and subtraction (SUB) mnemonics.

As you recall, the result from a specific operation is most often placed in the A register, or accumulator. The A register is named the accumulator mainly because the results of most operations are "accumulated" in this register. This register is also used as one of the sources of data for a calculation. For example, the mnemonic instruction ADD causes the system to add the contents of the A register to the contents of another register or memory location, and place the results back in the accumulator. The original contents of the accumulator are destroyed by the new data.

Figure 14-2 shows how the ADD instruction operates. Numerous instructions place the answer to arithmetic problems in the accumulator.

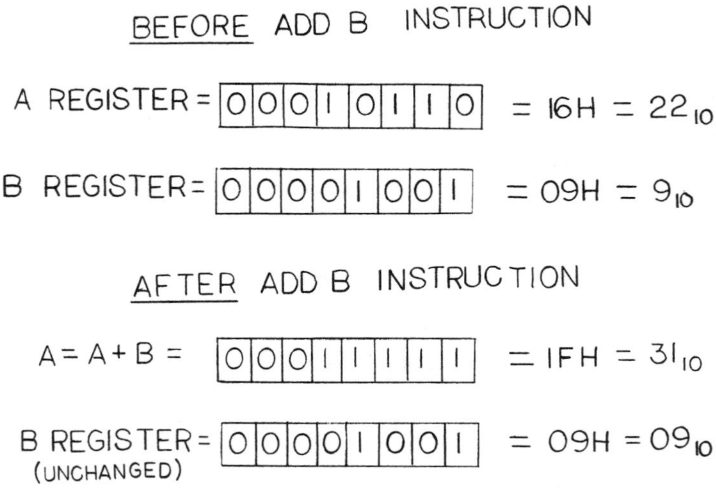

BEFORE ADD B INSTRUCTION

A REGISTER = | 0 | 0 | 0 | 1 | 0 | 1 | 1 | 0 | = 16H = 22_{10}

B REGISTER = | 0 | 0 | 0 | 0 | 1 | 0 | 0 | 1 | = 09H = 9_{10}

AFTER ADD B INSTRUCTION

A = A + B = | 0 | 0 | 0 | 1 | 1 | 1 | 1 | 1 | = 1FH = 31_{10}

B REGISTER = | 0 | 0 | 0 | 0 | 1 | 0 | 0 | 1 | = 09H = 09_{10}
(UNCHANGED)

FIGURE 14-2 Example of how the ADD instruction is executed by the 8080

Because the data word for the 8080 microprocessor is only 1 byte (8 bits) long, the range of valid numbers that can be represented is limited. If we were only concerned about positive integers, the range would be:

$$\text{minimum number} = 00000000_2 = 000_{10}$$
$$\text{maximum number} = 11111111_2 = 255_{10}$$

This scheme does not include a way of denoting negative numbers such that the microprocessor could distinguish them. A consistent method of representing negative and positive numbers simultaneously is the two's complement form. Figure 14-3 illustrates

STEP	OPERATION	DATA
1	DECIMAL FORM	2 2
2	HEXADECIMAL FORM	1 4
3	BINARY FORM	00010100
4	COMPLEMENT	11101011
5	$+1 = 2'S\ COMP = -22_{10}$	11101100

FIGURE 14-3   Forming the two's complement of a decimal number

the procedure used to form the two's complement form of a negative number. Note that the valid range of integers is now half as large as when using positive integers alone because the most significant bit is used to denote the sign of the number. For example, +1 = 00000001 and -1 = 11111111. The minimum and maximum valid two's complement values are now:

minimum number = -128_{10} = 10000000

maximum number = $+127_{10}$ = 01111111

To ensure that this number system is consistent, any number and its negative should add to zero. If 8_{10} and -8_{10} are added, the result is zero. Verify that this rule holds for any binary number arbitrarily chosen within the valid range that can be expressed by an 8 bit number. In general, we can say that the most positive number for a given field of x bits (for our system x=8 bits) is:

positive maximum = $(2^{x-1}) -1$

Similarly, the most negative number is given by the formula:

$$\text{negative maximum} = (2^{x-1})$$

What happens if the result of an operation exceeds the valid range of +127 and -128 in the case of the 8080? In other words, suppose we add +127 and +100. The result, $+227_{10}$, requires more than 8 bits to express in two's complement form (how many bits?). This is termed an overflow condition, and it must be checked for after each operation. Figure 14-4 summarizes the overflow conditions in adding two signed numbers.

SIGN OF:			HAS OVERFLOW OCCURRED ?
MEMORY DATA	ACCUMULATOR DATA	RESULT DATA	
+	+	+	NO
+	+	−	YES
+	−	±	NO
−	+	±	NO
−	−	−	NO
−	−	+	YES

FIGURE 14-4   Summary of two's complement arithmetic overflow conditions when adding data stored in memory to data in the A register(Accumulator)

Fortunately, there are five special 1-bit registers (flip-flops) called flags that indicate the condition of an addressed register after certain instructions. See Figure 14-5 for a summary of the 8080 flags. If we interrogate the flags at the right time, the validity of the data in the register in question can be determined.

As an example, suppose that after performing an ADD instruction the status of the Zero flag is checked and found to be set (set means to force the flag to a logical 1). This means that the contents of the accumulator now equals zero. Similarly, if the sign flag were set, the result in the accumulator must have its most significant bit set to a logical 1 to indicate a negative number is now in the accumulator. Access to

98

FIGURE 14-5 Summary of 8080 condition flags. For additional information
see Chapter 4 of the MCS-80 User's Manual.

ZERO (Z)	If the result of an instruction (affecting the zero flag) leaves the addressed register equal to 0, then the Z flag is set to logical 1. Otherwise, Z is reset to logical 0 with the completion of the instruction.
SIGN (S)	If the MSB (bit D7) of the data resulting from an operation (affecting the sign flag) is 0 (positive) then the S flag is reset to logical 0. Otherwise, (MSB=1=negative data) S is set to a logical 1.
PARITY (P)	If the sum of the logical 1 bits in the data resulting from an operation (affecting the parity flag) is even P is set to a logical 1. If the sum is odd , P is reset to a logical 0.
CARRY (CY)	The carry flag is set to a logical 1 if there is a carry into or out of the MSB of the data involved in the current operation (affecting the carry flag). If no carries occur CY is reset to a logical 0.
AUXILIARY (AC) CARRY	If a carry occurs from bit 3 to bit 4 in the current instruction (affecting the auxillary carry flag), AC is set to a logical 1. Otherwise, AC is reset to a logical 0. (See the DAA instruction in the MCS-80 User's Manual)

information in the flag registers is gained in one of two ways:
first, the bits can be directly examined through the Processor
Status Word (PSW) or second, the bits can be examined indirectly
by conditional branching. These techniques are explored in
Experiments 16 and 17, respectively.

OBJECTIVES

1. To understand the use of two's complement arithmetic,
and

2. To learn how to write arithmetic programs for the 8080
microprocessor.

INSTRUMENTS AND MATERIALS

1   8080 microprocessor training system

1   MCS-80 User's Manual

99

Recommended Reading: Reference 1
                          Pages 172-173

PROCEDURE

Step 1

The ADD and SUB instructions take numerous forms. Table 14-1A shows a representative summary of these mnemonics.

1.1   Review Table 14-1A and fill in the remaining entries. The first instruction is completed as an example.

1.2   Complete Table 14-1B for the increment and decrement instructions. These mnemonics effectively add or subtract 1 from a specified register or memory location. They perform in less time, using less memory than an ADI 01H instruction, for example.

Step 2

Now let us do some basic arithmetic in the two's complement system.

TABLE 14-1   Arithmetic instruction mnemonics for the 8080

	MNEMONIC	NUMBER OF BYTES	OP CODE (HEX)	OPERAND	FUNCTION
(A)	ADD	1	NUMEROUS	r	ADD CONTENTS OF r TO A REGISTER, PUT RESULT IN A REGISTER.
	ADC				
	ADI				
	ACI				
	SUB				
	SBB				
	SUI				
	SBI				
(B)	INR				
	INX				
	DCR				
	DCX				
	DAD				
	DAA				

2.1   Write an 8080 program that:

1.   Reads the data at memory location $00FF_{16}$

2.   Multiplies the data by -1 (take two's complement)

3.   Adds the new number to itself, and

4.   Writes the result to the system display.

2.2   Assemble, load, and run your program. Load memory locations $00FF_{16}$ with the following data:

Data	Data (in decimal)	Program Results
12_{16}		
31_{16}		
$0A_{16}$		
$8B_{16}$		

Predict your program for each value loaded at $00FF_{16}$. Do your predictions agree after the program is run? Explain why or why not.

2.3   Write a program that evaluates the following expression:

$$S = ((A + B) -C) -D$$

Assume A, B, C, and D are constants located in memory. Write the result (S) to the system display. Try various values for the constants and verify your predictions.

2.4   Rewrite your program of Step 2.3, using different mnemonics (instead of ADD M use ADI data, etc.). Assemble, load, and run this alternate program, using all negative data. Verify your results.

QUESTIONS

1.   What are the two largest equal positive numbers that can be added together in two's complement arithmetic?

2.   Summarize the conditions that will cause an invalid two's complement number when two valid two's complement integers are added together.   Repeat for the subtraction of two valid numbers.

3.   Express the following decimal numbers in two's complement form:

10	42
-32	-69
48	100
-23	-118

4.   Show five sets of two or three instructions that when executed will each set a different 8080 flag.   As an example:

MVI A, 00H

DCR A

will set the sign flag to logical 1.

5.   What additional status flag could be added to the 8080 to make arithmetic operations easier to check?

EXPERIMENT 15
BYTE AND BIT MANIPULATIONS

<u>DISCUSSION</u>

With data loaded into an internal register in the microprocessor (usually the accumulator), it is processed in some
manner. Processing may take the form of moving the bits or
bytes of the data word in a way that isolates portions of the
word for additional manipulations. When fractional parts of the
data word are isolated or considered by themselves they are
called fields. For example, if bits D7, D6, and D5 were to have
special significance they would form a three-bit field. The
isolation and subsequent use of these fields is the object of
this laboratory exercise.

The most common way to isolate a portion of an 8-bit data
word is through the use of the logical instructions that are
available with the 8080. We can also use rotate instructions
that cause the contents of the accumulator to be rotated left or
right by 1 bit. The three basic logical functions of interest
are the AND, OR, and EXCLUSIVE OR operations. Figure 15-1 gives
a capsule summary of these operations.

In order to examine the lower nibble (the 4 bits D3 to D0)
of an inputed data word, the upper bits (D7 to D4) must be
masked from consideration somehow. This is accomplished by
ANDing the word being considered with the data 00001111_2. Since
1 AND anything (1 or 0) is itself, the lower nibble (4 bits)
remains intact as the upper nibble is set to all zeroes. Remember, 0 AND anything is always 0. Once the upper 4 bits are
nulled or set to zero, the new word can be compared with some
known data to determine its value.

103

AND

INSTRUCTIONS- ANI
         ANA

A	DATA	RESULT
OO	OO	OO
OO	FF	OO
FF	OO	OO
FF	FF	FF

OR

INSTRUCTIONS- ORA
         ORI

A	DATA	RESULT
OO	O	OO
OO	FF	FF
FF	O	FF
FF	FF	FF

XOR

INSTRUCTIONS- XRA
         XRI

A	DATA	RESULT
OO	OO	OO
OO	FF	FF
FF	OO	FF
FF	FF	OO

FIGURE 15-1   Functional summary of ANA, ORA, and XRA instructions

Figure 15-2 summarizes this type of masking and other ways of setting a particular field to a desired value. In Figure 15-2, notice that:

A REG	DATA (HEX)	OPERATION (ON A REG)			
		ANI	ORI	XRI	COMMENT
ANY DATA	OO	OO	NO CHANGE	NO CHANGE	
ANY DATA	FF	FF	FF	COMPLE-MENT	
EXAMPLES					
AA	OO	OO	AA	AA	
AA	FF	FF	FF	55	
EE	OO	OO	EE	EE	
EE	FF	FF	FF	11	
.					

FIGURE 15-2   Summary of masking operations using Logical instructions. All instructions reference the Accumulator

104

1.   XRA A (Exclusive OR A with itself) sets the A register to zero. All flags are affected.

2.   ORA A (Inclusive OR A with itself) has no effect on the A register but does set or reset the appropriate flags.

3.   XRI FF (Exclusive OR A with all 1's) complements whatever data is presently in the A register.

4.   All logical instructions involve the A Register.

Besides affecting the data in the A register, the logical instructions also set or reset the appropriate flags.

OBJECTIVES

1.   To learn the use of the logical and rotate instructions of the 8080 microprocessor instruction set, and

2.   To develop some special software techniques for use in data field manipulations.

INSTRUMENTS AND MATERIALS

1   8080 microprocessor training system

1   8080 User's Manual

Recommended Reading: Reference 1
                           Pages 173-175

PROCEDURE

Step 1

Initially we need to review the instructions for processing bit fields in an 8080 microprocessor system.

1.1   Referring to the MCS-80 User's Manual, complete the chart shown in Figure 15-3. The first entry has been completed as an example.

1.2   Indicate the source code mnemonics that could be used to perform the following operations:

105

MNEMONIC	NUMBER OF BYTES	OP CODE (HEX)	OPERAND	FUNCTION
ANA	1	NUMEROUS	r	REGISTER r IS ANDED WITH THE A REGISTER.(A)←(A)•(r)
ANI				
ORA				
ORI				
XRA				
XRI				
CMP				
CPI				
RLC				
RRC				
RAL				
RAR				
CMA				
CMC				
STC				

FIGURE 15-3   Summmary of 8080 Logical instructions

1.   **NAND (NOT AND = the complement of the**

AND function)

2.   **NOR (NOT OR)**

Step 2

Now, we can apply these instructions and write a program.

2.1   The object of our program is to exchange the lower nibble with the upper nibble of the data word presently in a memory location called EXCHG. Load the data into the A register of the 8080 microprocessor and exchange the nibbles without using any external memory locations for temporary storage (use auxiliary registers). Any needed constants can be stored in memory, however. Once the exchange has been accomplished, output the result to an I/O port (preferably one where the data can be checked, as to the output display). Write a program that accomplishes this goal and assemble and load your program into the system.

2.2   Run the program and verify the results.

2.3   Rewrite your program using a different technique to accomplish the bit switching. Besides masking, the information can be rotated to accomplish the same goal. Consider using the rotate instructions shown in Figure 15-3.

2.4   Assemble, load, and run your second version and verify the results with the data AA_{16} and FF_{16} for EXCHG.

Step 3

A common situation where bit processing is required is in the identification of data as it is coming from a particular source. For example, suppose the processor is to examine bit D3 of the data coming from an I/O port until that bit goes to logical 1 state. When this happens the microprocessor is to signal the outside world by sending the data FF_{16} to a display port.

3.1   Write a program that will continually read the data at a known port address until bit D3 becomes a 1. When D3 becomes 1 the program is to output FF_{16} to another port or to the system display and halt. Include a flow chart with your solution.

3.2   Assemble and run the program in Step 3.1. How can you verify that the program is working in principal?

<u>Step 4</u>

Multiplication and division by 2 can be accomplished by the 8080 using the rotate left and rotate right instructions, respectively. As an example, if we wish to multiply 4_{10} by 2_{10}, load the A register with 04_{16} and rotate left by 1 bit. The source code for this operation is:

    MVI A, 04H

    RLC

4.1   Write a program that will evaluate the following:

    F = [(x+y)/4-1] [8]

Get the data x from a known I/O port and the data y from memory. Output the result to the display to check your program.

4.2   Assemble, load, and run the program of Step 3.1. Verify that your program works for these values of x and y:

x(HEX)	y(HEX)
04	1C
09	37
0F	08

How are fractions treated in this process? Can negative numbers be used for x and y?

<u>QUESTIONS</u>

1.   Show two ways of determining if bits D6, D4, D2 and D0 are set in a given data word.

2.   Can a data word be masked by making unwanted bits all zeros? Show a set of representative instructions.

108

3.   Does the 8080 contain any instructions that examine data fields or bits directly?

4.   Show the 8080 mnemonics that will set the carry flag (CY) to a logical 1, using both masking and rotating techniques.

5.   What are the limitations in multiplying and dividing by rotating the accumulator?

EXPERIMENT 16
USING THE STACK

DISCUSSION

A software concept used by many microprocessors involves the creation of a stack in the RAM memory area of the system. A stack is a portion of the read/write memory that is controlled by a specific group of instructions and is used to store data or addresses temporarily. The last data written to the stack is the first data that is read from the stack (LAST IN FIRST OUT format). The name "stack" is used because the data exists in a group of successive locations where new information is always placed at the top of existing data. Figure 16-1A shows how a

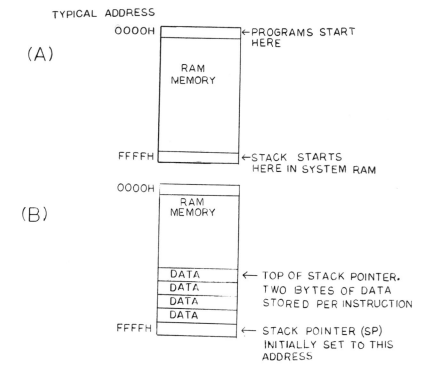

FIGURE 16-1   (A) Stack as it exists in the system RAM (B) Stack growing downward in the system RAM as the result of two PUSH instructions

110

stack exists in RAM.

The 8080 microprocessor allows any part of the RAM memory to be used for the stack. However, the first address of the stack is set generally at the highest address in memory, since the stack grows in a downward direction toward smaller addresses. Starting at a high address in memory does not waste any of the available RAM as programs will grow upward from lower addresses. Figure 16-1B illustrates this concept.

Two 8080 instructions that are used to manipulate the stack are:

PUSH rp   (Push or store the contents of register pair

                 (rp) onto the top of the stack)

POP rp   (Pop or remove the contents of register pair

                 rp off of the top of the stack)

We first note that these instructions involve register pairs (rp), or 16 bits of information. Consequently, entire addresses can be stored or retrieved from the stack with just a single instruction. As an example, if the PUSH B instruction is executed, the contents of the B and C registers, which could be an address, are placed on the stack as shown in Figure 16-2A. Similarly, if a POP B instruction is executed, the contents of the B and C registers are restored as indicated in Figure 16-2B.

Besides the PUSH and POP instructions, any 8080 memory reference instruction can access the stack. There is nothing illegal about reading or writing the stack portion of RAM with the LDA or STA instructions, for example. Care should be exercised, however, to ensure that data existing in the stack is kept in two byte groups to avoid confusing the data by entering in the wrong sequence.

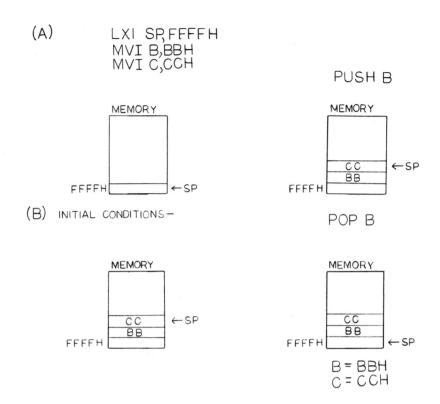

(A)   LXI SP,FFFFH
       MVI B,BBH
       MVI C,CCH

                                    PUSH B

       MEMORY   MEMORY

                                         CC ←SP
                                         BB
FFFFH ⌷   ⌷ ←SP   FFFFH ⌷   ⌷

(B) INITIAL CONDITIONS—   POP B

       MEMORY   MEMORY

         CC   ←SP   CC
         BB   BB
FFFFH ⌷   ⌷   FFFFH ⌷   ⌷ ←SP

                                  B = BBH
                                  C = CCH

FIGURE 16-2   (A) Register-pair BC written onto the Stack by a PUSH B
operation (B) Register-pair BC restored after a POP B instruction

    If the stack can exist in any valid RAM locations, how does
the microprocessor know where to begin and how to keep track of
data stored in the stack? This bookkeeping function is accomplished through the use of a special 16-bit address register
called the stack pointer or SP for short. The stack pointer
always contains the address of the next location in memory which
will be written into during stack operations. It must be initialized to some starting address before stack operations are
begun. This is accomplished by the LXI SP,data 16 instruction,

which is normally placed at the beginning of a program that uses the stack. It is the programmer's responsibility to initialize the stack pointer! Whenever a PUSH or POP instruction is used, the stack pointer is automatically incremented or decremented by two to point to the next valid stack location in memory. Two memory locations are always used in stack operations; this is why the stack pointer is changed by two.

In this experiment, we investigate the manipulation and use of the stack. As explained in Experiment 17, the stack can also be used to execute subroutines.

OBJECTIVES

1.   To understand how data or addresses can be temporarily stored and retrieved from the stack, and

2.   To learn the use of stack instructions.

INSTRUMENT AND MATERIALS

1   8080 microprocessor training system

1   MCS-80 User's Manual

        Recommended Reading: Reference 1
                                    Pages 175-179

PROCEDURE

Step 1

Data is normally stored on the stack in a sequential order. If we execute:

                        PUSH B

                        PUSH D

                        POP   D

                        POP   B

The original data in the BC and DE registers remains intact.

1.1   Write a short program using the PUSH and POP instructions that will exchange the contents of the D and E registers with the contents of the B and C registers through the stack. Load the two register pairs from memory and output the B register to the system display to verify your program results. Assemble, load, and run the program.

1.2   Modify the program of Step 1.1 to interchange the contents of the B and C registers before their data is exchanged with the D and E registers. Assemble, load, and run this program. What is the value of the SP when the program halts?

Step 2

An additional stack instruction is the PUSH PSW or POP PSW. The Processor Status Word (PSW) is 2 bytes of data that contain the current condition of the flags and the accumulator in the 8080. Figure 16-3 shows how the flags and accumulator data are encoded in the PSW.

2.1   Write a program that outputs the PSW to the system display and halts. Predict the values of the flags and verify your results. If your display holds only one byte at a time, output only the flag byte of the PSW.

2.2   Set the value of the first word of the PSW (accumulator) to 10101010_2. Output the PSW to the display (accumulator byte).

QUESTIONS

1.   Is there a maximum number of PUSH-POP instruction sequences that can be executed with the 8080? Explain why.

2.   If your system has 64K bytes of RAM and the currently

114

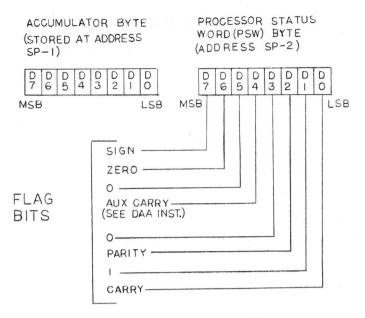

ACCUMULATOR BYTE
(STORED AT ADDRESS SP-1)

PROCESSOR STATUS WORD (PSW) BYTE
(ADDRESS SP-2)

FLAG BITS

SIGN
ZERO
0
AUX CARRY
(SEE DAA INST.)
0
PARITY
1
CARRY

FIGURE 16-3   Contents of the Processor Status Word (PSW) when pushed onto the Stack. See page 4-13 in the MCS-80 User's Manual for more information.

executing program requires 2K bytes of memory, how large a stack could be used?

3.   How many bytes of memory must all stack instructions require?   Include in your count the locations for the stack instruction itself.

4.   Where in memory can the SP be initialized to point? Could the SP be set to 0000_{16} initially?

5.   Write the source code to examine the contents of the SP while a program is executing. Note that the SP cannot be pushed into the stack, i.e., PUSH SP is an invalid instruction.

EXPERIMENT 17
CONDITIONAL JUMP INSTRUCTIONS

DISCUSSION

The real power of any microprocessor system comes from its ability to make decisions and act on the decision made. In the case of an 8080-based system, decisions are made by three groups of software instructions. These are the conditional jump, conditional call and conditional return groups. The conditional call and return groups are treated in Experiment 18. The goal of this experiment is the understanding of conditional jump instructions.

In Experiment 14, we were introduced to the 1-bit flag registers of the 8080. Besides being able to examine the status of the flags, the programmer can instruct the 8080 to jump to any desired location in memory based on the current condition of one or more of the flags.

Table 17-1 gives a summary of the conditional jump instructions available for the 8080. As an example, if a JP POS instruction were executed by the 8080, one of two possible actions would occur:

1. If the sign flag (S) were set to logical 1, the program counter in the 8080 would be set to an address named POS, causing the 8080 to jump to address POS and begin executing the instructions there.

2. If the sign flag were reset to logical 0, program execution would proceed normally with the next sequential instruction in memory - no jump would be performed.

The conditional instructions, themselves, do not affect the

TABLE 17-1   Summary of 8080 conditional JMP instructions. Note that all jump
instructions require 3 bytes; 1 byte for the OP-CODE and 2 bytes for the address
to jump to in memory.

MNEMONIC	NUMBER OF BYTES	OP CODE (HEX)	OPERAND	FUNCTION
JZ	3	CA	ADDRESS	Jump on zero flag= logical 1
JNZ	3	C2	"	Jump on zero flag= logical 0
JC	3	DA	"	Jump on carry flag= logical 1
JNC	3	D2	"	Jump on carry flag= logical 0
JP	3	F2	"	Jump on sign flag= logical 0
JM	3	FA	"	Jump on sign flag= logical 1
JPE	3	EA	"	Jump on parity flag= logical 1
JPO	3	E2	"	Jump on parity flag= logical 0
NOTES				

values of the flags. When a JP instruction is executed, the
value of the sign flag or any other flag is not altered. Numerous other instructions do affect the contents of the flags,
however. The exact position of a conditional instruction now
becomes very important.

For instance, consider the program in Figure 17-1A. Because the ANA B instruction affects the zero flag, it should not
be inserted between the DCR C and the conditional jump instruction. The object of the program in Figure 17-1A is to increase
the contents of the accumulator by 10_{10} and then halt. Since
the ANA B instruction follows the DCR C instruction used as a
loop counter the program will count to 255 before halting. A
correct solution to the problem is shown in Figure 17-1B. Here

117

the value of the sign flag reflects the current loop counter when the conditional jump instruction is encountered.

```
 1 0000                  ****************************************************
 2 0000                  *                                                  *
 3 0000                  *            INCORRECT PROGRAM EXAMPLE              *
 4 0000                  *                                                  *
 5 0000                  ****************************************************
 6 0000 3E 00                  MVI A,00H      /CLEAR A REGISTER
 7 0002 06 01                  MVI B,01H      /INITIALIZE B REGISTER TO 1
 8 0004 0E 0A                  MVI C,0AH      /SET C REGISTER TO 10
 9 0006 0D           LOOP      DCR C          /DECREASE THE C REGISTER BY 1
10 0007 A0                     ANA B          /ADD 1 TO THE A REGISTER
11 0008 C2 06 00               JNZ LOOP       /GO BACK TO LOOP IF ZERO FLAG=0
12 000B 76                     HLT
13 000C                        END

     0 ERRORS              1 SYMBOLS

 1 0000                  ****************************************************
 2 0000                  *                                                  *
 3 0000                  *             CORRECT PROGRAM EXAMPLE              *
 4 0000                  *                                                  *
 5 0000                  ****************************************************
 6 0000 3E 00                  MVI A,00H      /CLEAR A REGISTER
 7 0002 06 01                  MVI B,01H      /INITIALIZE B REGISTER TO 1
 8 0004 0E 0A                  MVI C,0AH      /SET C REGISTER TO 10
 9 0006 A0           LOOP      ANA B          /ADD 1 TO THE A REGISTER
10 0007 3D                     DCR A          /DECREASE THE C REGISTER BY 1
11 0008 C2 06 00               JNZ LOOP       /GO BACK TO LOOP IF ZERO FLAG=0
12 000B 76                     HLT
13 000C                        END

     0 ERRORS              1 SYMBOLS
```

FIGURE 17-1 Examples of 8080 programs using flags incorrectly and correctly

The JNZ and JZ instructions are often used to write timing loops. A timing loop is a set of instructions that is used to slow down the activities of a microprocessor. An application would be the use of a timing loop between I/O write operations to the display port. This would provide time, say 2 seconds, for the display to be read visually by the programmer before new data is written. Figure 17-2 shows a typical timing loop sub-routine where the contents of memory locations WAITA and WAITB determine the length of program delay. This program is analyzed in the procedure section.

During this experiment, we consider some of the uses of conditional jump instructions and common problems encountered in their application.

	ADDRESS	OBJECT CODE	LABEL	OP-CODE	OPERAND	COMMENTS
4	0000H			XRA	A	/CLEAR A REGISTER
10			NEXT	OUT	00H	/OUTPUT CONTENTS OF A
17				CALL	WAIT	/GOTO WAIT ROUTINE
5				INR	A	/INCREASE (A)
10				JMP	NEXT	/CONTINUE
7			WAIT	MVI	B,WAITA	/GET VALUE OF DELAY
7				MVI	C,WAITB	/GET VALUE OF DELAY
5			LOOP	DCR	B	/DECREASE B BY 1
10				JNZ	LOOP	/
5				DCR	C	
10				JNZ LOOP		/CONTINUE
10				RET		/RETURN TO MAIN PROG
			WAITA	EQU	FFH	/SET WAITA EQUAL TO FFH
			WAITB	EQU	FFH	/SET WAITB EQUAL TO FFH

FIGURE 17-2   Time delay subroutine(unassembled)

OBJECTIVES

1. To become familiar with all of the jump condition instructions available on the 8080, and

2. To understand and write some representative programs, using the conditional jump mnemonics.

INSTRUMENTS AND MATERIALS

1   8080 microprocessor training system

1   MCS-80 User's Manual

Recommended Reading: Reference 1
                           Pages 180-189

119

```
PROGRAM SEGMENTS

(A)  AGAIN   MVI   A,FOH    /LOAD A REGISTER
             DCR   A        /SUBTRACT 1 FROM A REGISTER
             JM    AGAIN    /GOTO AGAIN
             HLT

(B)  AGAIN   MVI   A,FOH
             DCR   A
             JNC   AGAIN
             HLT

(C)  AGAIN   MVI   A,FOH
             DCR   A
             JPO   AGAIN
             HLT

(D)  AGAIN   MVI   A,F9H
             DCR   A
             JNZ   AGAIN
             HLT
```

FIGURE 17-3   Conditional JMP instruction program segments

```
PROGRAM SEGMENTS

(A)  AGAIN   MVI   A,FOH    /LOAD A
             DCR   A        /DECREASE A BY 1
             JP    AGAIN    /GOTO AGAIN
             HLT

(B)  AGAIN   MVI   A,FOH
             DCR   A
             JC    AGAIN
             HLT

(C)  AGAIN   MVI   A,FOH
             DCR   A
             JPE   AGAIN
             HLT

(D)  AGAIN   MVI   A,FOH
             DCR   A
             JZ    AGAIN
             HLT
```

FIGURE 17-4   More conditional JMP program segments

PROCEDURE

Step 1

Consider the program segments shown in Figures 17-3 and 17-4.

1.1   For each program segment determine the contents of the accumulator and the flags when the program halts. Complete Table 17-2 with your results.

1.2   Add to each program segment in Figures 17-3 and 17-4 the instructions shown in Figure 17-5. What is the purpose of these additional instructions? Be sure to place the instructions of Figure 17-5 in an appropriate order.

1.3   Assemble, load, and run each of the programs generated in Step 1.2. Verify that the results predicted in

Step 1.1 agree with your program's outputs.

TABLE 17-2 Contents of the Accumulator and the flags after the program segments in FIGURES 17-3 and 17-4 are executed. If the contents are unknown write a ?.

| PROGRAM SEGMENT | ACCUMULATOR (IN HEX) | FLAGS (∅OR1) | | | | | COMMENTS |
		S	Z	P	CY	AC	
17-3 A							
17-3 B							
17-3 C							
17-3 D							
17-4 A							
17-4 B							
17-4 C							
17-4 D							

Step 2

We now write a program that exercises your understanding of the 8080 flags.

ADDRESS	OBJECT CODE				LABEL	OP-CODE	OPERAND	COMMENTS
						LXI	SP,FFFFH	/INITIALIZE SP
						PUSH	PSW	/PUSH PSW ONTO STACK
						LDA	FFFEH	/GET PSW FROM STACK
						OUT	PORT	/SEND TO SYSTEM DISPLAY
					PORT	EQU	00H	/SET PORT EQUAL TO 00H

FIGURE 17-5 Software to output the PSW to the system display (Port 00H)

2.1   Review the following arithmetic expression:

X = ((A+B)+C)*2

2.2   Write a program that evaluates the expression in Step 2.1 under the following conditions:

121

1.   Assume that A, B and C are all valid 8-bit two's complement integers (+127 to -128).

2.   Using the overflow chart in Figure 14-4, evaluate the expression of Step 2.1, halt if any operation is invalid, and display FF_{16} in the system display.

3.   If all operations are valid, display the value of X and halt.

2.3   Assemble, load, and run the program of Step 2.2. Enter the following values to verify your program:

A	B	C
128_{10}	128_{10}	0_{10}
35_{10}	78_{10}	99_{10}
1_{10}	1_{10}	2_{10}

Which of these sets of data would yield an FF_{16} in the system display?

Step 3

3.1   Review the timing loop shown in Figure 17-2. Determine the tcy of your system by examining your system operating manual or by direct measurement of Phase 1.

3.2   To the far left of each instruction in Figure 17-2 is a number equal to the total tcy's that the 8080 requires to execute that instruction. Write an equation that expresses how long the 8080 would take to execute the timing loop program. Assume WAITA = WAITB = FF_{16}.

total time (in seconds) = _____

3.3   Set WAITA = WAITB = FF_{16}. Assemble, load, and run the program in Figure 17-2. Time the program's execution to verify your calculations in Step 3.2.

3.4   Rewrite the timing program so that an exact wait

of 30 seconds is achieved. Assemble, load, and run to verify your program.

QUESTIONS

1. How many possible conditional jump instructions are available for the 8080 microprocessor?

2. Is there any flag that can be checked to verify that an arithmetic operation is valid? (under two's complement arithmetic)

3. Could a conditional jump instruction jump to a memory location in the system's ROM? What would happen?

4. What is the maximum resolution that can be achieved using the timing loop in Step 3? What are the minimum and maximum wait times for this program?

5. What instructions affect the Auxiliary Carry (AC) flag in the 8080? Under what conditions is this flag important?

6. List five instructions that do not affect the 8080 flags.

EXPERIMENT 18
SUBROUTINES

DISCUSSION

The amount of RAM memory that is available in most micro-processor systems is limited. Without using elaborate techniques, an 8080-based system is limited to 65,536 addressable memory locations (1 byte/location). Because of this size limitation and memory cost considerations, most programs are written to be as small as possible. In other words, to perform a given task, the smaller the program (in terms of bytes), the better. One common technique used to reduce program size is to structure a program with subroutines. A subroutine is a set of instructions that can be executed from anywhere in a program, any number of times. The understanding and use of subroutines is the goal of this experiment.

Figure 18-1 shows the program sequence in executing a subroutine. In order for the microprocessor to know where to return to in memory after a subroutine is executed, the return address must be saved somewhere in the system. We define the return address as the next location in memory that the CPU reads and executes after completing a subroutine. This return address is saved on the stack automatically when a CALL instruction is executed. The 8080 retrieves the return address from the stack by executing a RET instruction, which is normally the last instruction in any subroutine. The RET instruction, therefore, POPs the return address off the stack. This technique for saving and restoring the return address makes possible the nesting of subroutines. A nested subroutine is one that is called from another subroutine.

124

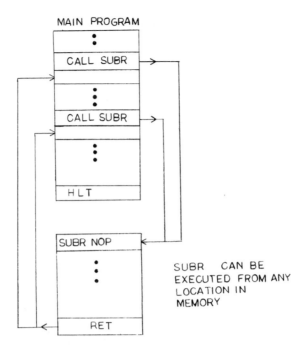

FIGURE 18-1   Program flow in executing a subroutine

The CALL and RET instructions also exist as conditional statements in the 8080. This means that the programmer can make a decision to call a subroutine or return from one based on the current status of the internal 8080 flags without using additional instructions. As an example, if a subroutine were being used to count down to zero from some initial value, the RZ instruction could be used at the end of the subroutine as a test for the return condition. Figure 18-2 a summarizes the conditional call and conditional return instructions.

With the completion of this experiment the reader should have a good understanding of the role that subroutines play in software design.

MNEMONIC	NUMBER OF BYTES	OP CODE (HEX)	OPERAND	FUNCTION
RNZ	3	C0	ADDRESS	RETURN WHEN Z=0;OTHERWISE EXECUTE NEXT INST.
RZ	3	C8	ADDRESS	RETURN WHEN Z=1;OTHERWISE EXECUTE NEXT INST.
RNC	3	D0	ADDRESS	RETURN WHEN CY=0
RC	3	D8	ADDRESS	RETURN WHEN CY=1
RPO	3	E0	ADDRESS	RETURN WHEN P=0
RPE	3	E8	ADDRESS	RETURN WHEN P=1
RP	3	F0	ADDRESS	RETURN WHEN S=0
RM	3	F8	ADDRESS	RETURN WHEN S=1
CNZ	3	C4	ADDRESS	CALL SUBROUTINE WHEN Z=0
CZ	3	CC	ADDRESS	CALL SUBROUTINE WHEN Z=1
CNC	3	D4	ADDRESS	CALL SUBROUTINE WHEN CY=0
CC	3	DC	ADDRESS	CALL SUBROUTINE WHEN CY=1
CPO	3	E4	ADDRESS	CALL SUBROUTINE WHEN P=0
CPE	3	EC	ADDRESS	CALL SUBROUTINE WHEN P=1
CP	3	F4	ADDRESS	CALL SUBROUTINE WHEN S=0
CM	3	FC	ADDRESS	CALL SUBROUTINE WHEN S=1

FIGURE 18-2   Summary of conditional RET and conditional CALL instructions

OBJECTIVES

1.   To understand the uses and advantages of subroutines, and

2.   To learn the details of how subroutines are managed by the 8080.

INSTRUMENTS AND MATERIALS

1   8080 microprocessor training system

1   MCS-80 User's Manual

Recommended Reading: Reference 1
Pages 180-181

PROCEDURE

Step 1

The first step in understanding subroutines is to investigate how the microprocessor keeps track of return addresses.

1.1   Assemble, load, and run the program shown in Figure 18-3A. This program calls a subroutine named SUB1 and halts while in the subroutine.

(A)

ADDRESS	OBJECT CODE			LABEL	OP-CODE	OPERAND	COMMENTS
0000H					XRA	A	/SET A REGISTER TO 0
					MOV	B,A	/SET B REGISTER TO 0
					OUT	00H	/CLEAR DISPLAY (port00H)
					CALL	SUB1	/CALL SUBROUTINE SUB1
					INR	A	/
					OUT	00H	/
					HLT		/
				SUB1	INR	A	/BEGIN SUB1
					OUT	00H	
					HLT		

(B)

					OP-CODE	OPERAND	COMMENTS
					ANI	A,00H	/CLEAR ACCUMULATOR
					MVI	B,00H	/CLEAR B REGISTER
					OUT	00H	/CLEAR DISPLAY
					CALL	SUB1	/GO TO SUB1
					INR	A	/INCREASE A BY 1
					OUT	00H	/SEND TO DISPLAY
					HLT		
				SUB1	INR	A	/INCREMENT A BY 1
					OUT	00H	/OUTPUT TO DISPLAY
					RET		/RETURN TO MAIN PROG.

FIGURE 18-3   (A) Subroutine example without a RET instruction (B) Subroutine example with normal termination (RET instruction)

1.2   Verify that the return address in the main program is now on the stack. Use the memory examination techniques of your system. Make sure that the stack pointer is initialized to a valid area of the RAM in your system.

1.3   Assemble, load, and run the program in Figure

18-3B. Note that a RET instruction has been added to SUB1 and that the microprocessor now halts in the main program rather than in SUB1.

1.4   Examine the stack locations in memory and verify that the return address is still stored in the stack. Because the stack is used to store return addresses, care must be taken when using PUSH and POP instructions while in a subroutine. If a PUSH were executed without a POP during the subroutine, the microprocessor would use the pushed data as a return address!

Step 2

Subroutines can be called from other subroutines, which is commonly called "nesting". The number of times that the nesting occurs dictates how deeply the subroutines are nested. Now we will examine a nesting that is two deep.

2.1   Consider the subroutine in Step 1.3. Add a call to SUB2 at the first line of SUB1. Write a subroutine called SUB2 that outputs 11_{16} to the system display and halts. Assemble, load, and run your program.

2.2   Now, assemble, load, and run the program shown in Figure 18-4. Verify that the contents of the stack contain the

ADDRESS	OBJECT CODE			LABEL	OP-CODE	OPERAND	COMMENTS
0000H					XRA	A	/SET A TO 0
					MVI	B,00H	/SET B TO 0
					OUT	00H	/OUTPUT TO PORT 00H
					CALL	SUB1	/GO TO SUB1
					INR	A	/INCREASE A BY 1
					OUT	00H	/OUTPUT TO DISPLAY
					HLT		/STOP
				SUB1	INR	A	/SET A=02H
					OUT	00H	/OUTPUT A TO DISPLAY
					CALL	SUB2	/GO TO SUB2
					RET		/RETURN TO MAIN PROG
				SUB2	NOP		/ENTRY TO SUB2
					HLT		

FIGURE 18-4   Main program and subroutines for example in the procedure

return addresses to SUB1 and SUB2 when the program halts.

Step 3

Now we examine the conditional return instructions.

3.1   Using the conditional return instructions, write
two subroutines that could be called in the sequence shown in
Figure 18-4. The subroutines are to do the following:

SUBRA: Count down from 100_{10} to 0 and return.

SUBRB: Count up from 0 until a negative number
            is reached (80_{16}) and return.

3.2   Assemble, load, and run the program written in
Step 3.1. How can you verify that your program works?

3.3   Rewrite SUBRA and SUBRB so that they output the
Processor Status Word (PSW) to the system display and wait 1
second each time a count is incremented or decremented. Use a
wait loop in a subroutine for the delay of 1 second (time enough
to read the display).

3.4   Assemble, load, and run the program written in
Step 3.3. Verify that the subroutines are working as antici-
pated.

Step 4

Finally, we investigate the conditional call instructions.

4.1   Write a subroutine that outputs whatever is in
the B register when it is called. Name the subroutine OUTB.
The contents of the accumulator are to remain intact (temporarily save the A register).

4.2   Using a conditional call instruction, write a
main program that performs the operations shown in Figure 18-5.
Use OUTB for writing data to the system display.

129

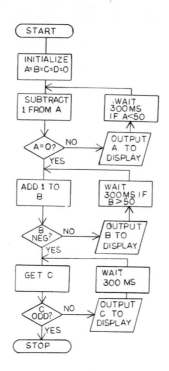

FIGURE 18-5   Flow chart of a conditional CALL program

4.3   Assemble, load, and run the program written in Step 4.2. Verify your program's operation.

QUESTIONS

1.   Name two reasons for using subroutines.

2.   Show how the RZ, RP, RM, CNZ, CNC and CPE instructions could be replaced with other 8080 instructions that would perform the same function.

3.   When would a two-line subroutine like the following be of value?

DCR A

RET

4.   When shouldn't POP and PUSH instructions be used in a

130

subroutine?

5.   If the allotted space for the stack in a system were 9 bytes of RAM, how deeply could the system subroutines be nested?

EXPERIMENT 19
TROUBLESHOOTING MEMORIES

<u>DISCUSSION</u>

Troubleshooting a malfunctioning microprocessor system usually involves close examination of one or more of the basic system blocks. This experiment deals with techniques and procedures necessary to find and repair hardware faults in the memory portion of the system.

If any portion of the system memory is functioning, then limited size programs can be loaded into that section and used to check out the remaining portions of memory. Such programs that are used to evaluate system hardware are called <u>diagnostic</u> programs. Their function is to exercise the hardware and evaluate the resulting output. As an example, a memory diagnostic program writes a pattern of known bits into RAM and then reads them back, comparing the read-back data against what was initially written. If any differences are discovered during this process, the program will take some action such as writing the defective address to the system display, and halting.

Numerous types of patterns can be devised to check whether the system memory is sensitive to the pattern of bits that is stored in it. Figure 19-1 summarizes some common memory data patterns that can be used for a 4-bit memory.

The kinds of errors that are encountered when checking semiconductor memories come in two types. If a particular location in memory is <u>always</u> inoperative, it is termed a "hard" error. If the failure occurs intermittently, it is called a "soft" error. Since both types of memory problems can occur, it

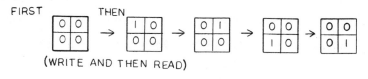

FIRST   THEN

(WRITE AND THEN READ)

(B)

(C)

(D)

FIGURE 19-1   4 examples of memory diagnostic patterns for a 4 bit memory

is good practice to cycle diagnostic programs several times to check for soft errors that might occur after the first pass, during which it might not reveal itself.

How do we determine if enough memory is working so that a diagnostic program can be used? To check the memory initially, the SST can be used. The large number of memory locations makes such testing very tedious by hand. Therefore, a reasonable procedure is to verify only enough of the memory to hold a diagnostic program first, then load and run the program to check the rest of the memory.

In this experiment, we write, assemble, load, and run a diagnostic program as would be done in a real troubleshooting situation. After some program enhancements, we introduce a

known hardware fault and check that the diagnostic program
identifies the problem. Finally, we recheck the introduced
fault with the SST as an additional verification. Figure 19-2
shows a generalized flowchart for troubleshooting external
signals presented to a memory device.

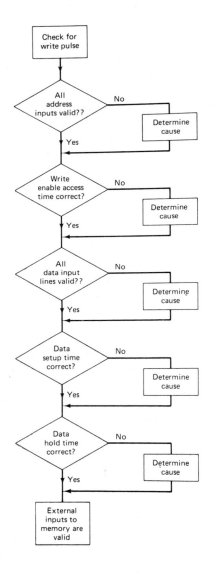

FIGURE 19-2   Memory diagnostic flow chart used in troubleshooting memories

<u>OBJECTIVES</u>

1.   To develop techniques for writing memory diagnostic programs

2.   To learn how to apply the SST to check and verify a portion of the system memory initially, and

3.   To assemble, load, and run a diagnostic program on a faulted system.

<u>INSTRUMENTS AND MATERIALS</u>

1   8080 microprocessor training system

1   MCS-80 User's Manual

1   Static Stimulus Tester

1   Logic probe or DVM

    Recommended Reading: Reference 1
                               Pages 53-59, 226-233

<u>PROCEDURE</u>

   <u>Step 1</u>

   First, we examine a representative memory diagnostic program.

   1.1   Study the source code for the memory diagnostic program shown in Figure 19-3. Make any changes in the program necessary for it to write to locations in memory that are defined as RAM for your system. What will this program accomplish?

   1.2   Load the object code of the program examined in Step 1.1 and verify that the program works on your system (run the program).

   <u>Step 2</u>

   Now that a diagnostic program has been run we will expand

135

```
 1 0000                  *****************************************************
 2 0000                  *
 3 0000                  *             MEMORY DIAGNOSTIC PROGRAM
 4 0000                  *
 5 0000                  *    THIS PROGRAM WILL EXAMINE A SELECTED PORTION OF THE
 6 0000                  *    SYSTEM RAM MEMORY, LOOKING FOR THE PATTERN BYTE
 7 0000                  *    STORED IN THE B REGISTER.  THE PATTERN BYTE IS
 8 0000                  *    DISPLAYED WHILE THE PROGRAM EXECUTES. MEMORY LOCATION
 9 0000                  *    0700 IS USED TO STORE THE NUMBER OF TIMES THE PATTERN
10 0000                  *    BYTE WAS FOUND.
11 0000                  *
12 0000                  *****************************************************
13 0000                  *
14 0000
15 0000 11 30 07             LXI D,0730H   /INITIALIZE D REGISTER TO START OF RAM T
16 0003 21 00 01             LXI H,0100H   /INITIALIZE H AND L TO START OF RAM TO C
17 0006 0E 00               MVI C,00H      /SET C REGISTER TO 0
18 0008 06 AA               MVI B,0AAH     /INITIALIZE B REGISTER = PATTERN BYTE =
19 000A 78                  MOV A,B        /MOVE PATTERN BYTE TO A REGISTER.
20 000B D3 00               OUT 00H        /WRITE PATTERN BYTE TO DISPLAY(SELECT CO
21 000D BE          AGAIN   CMP M          /LOOK FOR PATTERN AT FIRST RAM LOCATION.
22 000E CC 22 00            CZ HIT         /IF THE PATTERN IS THERE, JUMP TO SUBROU
23 0011 2C                  INR L          /INCREMENT L REGISTER TO POINT TO NEXT W
24 0012 C2 0D 00            JNZ AGAIN      /IF NOT LAST WORD JUMP TO AGAIN.
25 0015 EB                  XCHG           /GET THE REGISTER PAIR DE.
26 0016 36 00               MVI M,00H      /WRITE 00 BREG 00 TO THE END OF THE LIST
27 0018 2C                  INR L
28 0019 70                  MOV M,B
29 001A 2C                  INR L
30 001B 36 00               MVI M,00H
31 001D 79                  MOV A,C        /STORE NUMBER OF FOUND PATTERN BYTES AT
32 001E 32 00 07            STA 0700H
33 0021 76                  HLT            /STOP WHEN FINISHED
34 0022            *
35 0022            *
36 0022            *****************************************************
37 0022            *
38 0022            *              SUBROUTINE HIT
39 0022            *
40 0022            *****************************************************
41 0022            *
42 0022            *
43 0022 0C         HIT     INR C          /INCREMENT PATTERN BYTE COUNTER
44 0023 EB                  XCHG           /GET REGISTER PAIR DE
45 0024 73                  MOV M,E        /MOVE ADDRESS OF FOUND PATTERN BYTE TO M
46 0025 2C                  INR L          /POINT TO NEXT ADDRESS IN FOUND PATTERN
47 0026 EB                  XCHG           /GET REGISTER PAIR HL BACK
48 0027 C9                  RET            /UNCONDITIONAL RETURN TO MAIN PROGRAM.
49 0028            *
50 0028            *
51 0028            *****************************************************
52 0028            *
53 0028            *              SUBROUTINE   WRITE
54 0028            *
55 0028            *****************************************************
56 0028            *
57 0028            *
58 0028            *
59 0028 0E FF               MVI C,0FFH     /INITIALIZE C REGISTER TO 1 PAGE (256 L
60 002A 78                  MOV A,B
61 002B 77         NEXT    MOV M,A        /WRITE PATTERN BYTE TO MEMORY
62 002C 2C                  INR L          /POINT TO NEXT MEMORY LOCATION.
63 002D 0D                  DCR C          /DECREMENT LOOP COUNTER
64 002E CA 2B 00            JZ NEXT        /CHECK FOR END OF RAM
65 0031 C9                  RET            /UNCONDITIONAL RETURN
66 0032                     END
```

     0 ERRORS   3 SYMBOLS

FIGURE 19-3   Memory diagnostic program

the capabilities of the program to provide us with more information.

2.1   Rewrite the program of Step 1 so that it:

1.   Outputs the address of the first location found
to be defective

2.   Writes a pattern of 101010101, etc., into the
memory area to be checked, and

3.   Displays a 77_{16} if all locations are good after
the memory has been checked.

2.2   Assemble, load, and run the program of Step 2.1
and check your results.

2.3   Very carefully remove one of the RAM memory ICs
from your system and bend a single address lead away from the
body of the IC. Reinsert the memory IC in its socket. Now,
based on which address pin was disconnected, predict the first
location in memory where the diagnostic program should fail.
Run your program and check your prediction.

Step 3

Now we try some additional patterns of data for the diagnostic program to write to memory.

3.1   Modify the source code of the program written in
Step 2 to generate one of the alternative data patterns shown in
Figure 19-1.

3.2   Assemble, load, and run the program on your
trainer. Verify the expected results. (Make sure you have
reconnected the address pin that was disconnected in Step 2).

Step 4

Up to this point, we have assumed that an area of memory
large enough for the diagnostic program exists and operates in

the system memory. If this were not the case, some means has to be provided to check the small area in the memory initially required, and verify that it works.

4.1   How many locations of memory does the program written in Step 2 use in your system?

Number of memory locations = _____ 10.

4.2   Connect the SST to your system following the procedure of Experiment 4.

4.3   Using the write sequence of events discussed in Experiment 4, write a logical 1 into every bit in the memory where the diagnostic program would reside.

4.4   Using the SST, read each of the locations written in Step 4.3. If the data is not all 1's at any of the memory locations, use the flow chart in Figure 19-2 to isolate the problem.

4.5   Repeat Steps 4.3 and 4.4, but this time use logical 0 as the write and expect data. Unless the memory has a dynamic or pattern sensitivity problem, the system should verify that it is operating and is ready for the diagnostic program to be loaded and run.

QUESTIONS

1.   List all the hardware faults that you can think of that would cause a system memory malfunction.

2.   Should a memory diagnostic program be as long or as short as possible? Why?

3.   Would a memory diagnostic program for a ROM memory be of any practical use? What kinds of operations would such a program perform?

4. Draw a flow chart that gives the order of events in troubleshooting a microprocessor system memory (RAM or ROM).

5. How many times approximately should a diagnostic program write and read data to memory in your system? Express your answer in number of write-reads per bit.

6. If a memory location were "stuck" half way between logical 1 and logical 0, would the diagnostic program of Step 2 find this condition?

EXPERIMENT 20
TROUBLESHOOTING I/O PORTS

<u>DISCUSSION</u>

In this experiment we isolate the problems that occur when data is transferred between a microprocessor and the outside world (I/O ports). The four major causes for failure of an I/O operation are:

1. Bus contentions or conflicts

2. Buffer drive failures

3. Decoding faults

4. Local timing problems

Bus contentions arise when two or more active devices in a system try to control a bus at precisely the same time. For example, if two input ports are enabled at the same time, they both try to force data onto the system data bus. Since the data coming from one port is probably not the same as data coming from another port, the final state of the bus is uncertain. Bus contentions are possible on nearly any shared bus line (address, data, or control).

Additionally, the buffers that drive the buses may become weak or may malfunction to the point where they can no longer provide enough current to drive the entire bus load adequately. If logic voltage levels at the buffer outputs are found to be out of specification, this is often a clue to such a loading problem.

Each I/O port in a system must have a unique address or port select code. The successful decoding of this address is crucial if the port is to function at all. When a specific port in the system is malfunctioning, one should suspect the port enable signal(s) generated by the port decode logic as a first source of the fault.

The last general area that causes problems with I/O is the signal timing at the port. Local timing problems are not usually found by static stimulus testing. In most cases, the microprocessor allows adequate time margins between active signals. However, if these signals are slowed relative to each other by propagation delays introduced at the port, a variety of problems can occur. Even though the system has worked in the past, the aging of the integrated circuits in the system can cause a shift in signal delays to the point of malfunction. Such shifts are usually allowed for by the system designer, but a defective IC can exceed any allowances made. Sometimes, problems and oversights in the initial design may cause timing problems. Troubleshooting these and more elaborate timing problems are best addressed with sophisticated diagnostic tools like logic analyzers and in-circuit emulation systems. However, the majority of problems encountered in I/O troubleshooting of any well-designed system are static in nature and are not timing problems, so we will not address timing problems in this experiment.

By introducing known faults into the system's I/O structure, we can develop a method for locating an I/O fault using the SST and simple diagnostic programs.

OBJECTIVES

1. To learn common hardware problems arising in I/O circuits, and

2.   To develop a standard approach to troubleshooting I/O ports.

INSTRUMENTS AND MATERIALS

1   8080 microprocessor training system

1   Logic probe or oscilloscope

1   Set of system schematics

Recommended Reading: Reference 1
                        Pages 212-226

PROCEDURE

Step 1

Initially, we examine a selected I/O port, using a simple diagnostic program.

1.1   Review the I/O ports in your system and choose an appropriate output port.

Port select code = _____2

1.2   Assemble, load, and run the following simple program:

        Start   MVI A, 88H

                 OUT PORT

                 JMP START

        Note: PORT = port select code

1.3   Referring to the schematic for the port chosen in Part 1.1, locate the output of the port address decode circuitry. Using a logic probe, check that this pin is now active. (The logic probe should blink).

1.4   Verify that the address and data buses are also active. Can you be sure that all address and data lines are changing state?

1.5   Decrease the value of the select code used in Step 1.2 by one. Reassemble, load, and run the program of Step 1.2 with this new value.

1.6   Using a logic probe, verify that the port address decode output is now inactive and data is not getting to this port.

Step 2

If the diagnostic program fails, we still don't know precisely what is causing the failure. Is the decode circuitry malfunctioning, or is the port address just not getting to the circuitry? For an answer we apply the SST.

2.1   Remove the 8080 from your system and install the SST as outlined in Experiment 4.

2.2   Perform an I/O write to the port chosen in Step 1.1. Verify that the data arrives at this port and is latched.

2.3   Again enter the I/O write as in Step 2.2, but this time change the select code while monitoring the decode logic output. The output should be active only for the correct port address.

2.4   Verify that I/OW is active at the port during the write operation.

QUESTIONS

1. List three common I/O faults.

2. How many I/O addresses are possible in an 8080 system?

3. Draw a schematic for an I/O port decoder with a select code of FD_{16}.

4. What kinds of I/O decoding are used in microprocessor systems?

EXPERIMENT 21

EXAMINING MICROPROCESSOR WAVEFORMS

DISCUSSION

In this final experiment, we investigate the microprocessor system while operating it in a dynamic state. The system is examined while a program is being executed repeatedly by the microprocessor. If we restrict the program size, the same system signals reoccur periodically, to the point of allowing direct examination with an oscilloscope. Otherwise, a more sophisticated means of dynamic system analysis is required, such as a logic state analyser.

In Experiment 9, we learned that most microprocessor systems are driven by a free-running clock. Each software instruction of the 8080 is executed in a fixed number of free-running clock cycles. Figure 21-1 shows the relationship between the system clocks and the execution of an OUT instruction (chosen

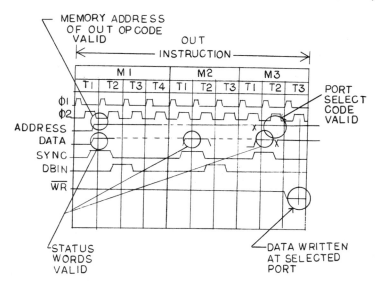

FIGURE 21-1   Relationship between system clocks and control signals during an OUT instruction

144

arbitrarily).   Since the SYNC signal occurs uniquely at the
beginning of every machine cycle, we can use it as a trigger for
the oscilloscope when viewing other system signals.   The events
that occur during each machine cycle are not unique.   However,
if we use a single instruction program, a unique repetitive
instruction cycle will occur.

This experiment provides an opportunity to compare the ease
and speed of static stimulus testing to troubleshooting dynam-
ically with an oscilloscope.

OBJECTIVES

1.   To observe 8080 signals while the system is operating,
and

2.   To examine and understand the problems and limitations
associated with viewing system signals directly via the oscilloscope.

INSTRUMENTS AND MATERIALS

1   8080 microprocessor training system

1   Oscilloscope, dual channel (4 channel if possible)
     with probes

1   MCS-80 User's Manual

     Recommended Reading: Reference 1
                                   Pages 112-141

PROCEDURE

Step 1

The smallest program that can execute continuously in an
8080 system is:

                HERE   JMP   HERE

where HERE is a label identifying the memory location of the jump instruction OP-CODE (JMP). This program will continuously jump to itself and, by running this smallest program, a relatively small amount of information can be transferred around the system.

1.1   Assemble and load the JMP HERE program into the user RAM area of your system.

1.2   Connect the external trigger input of the oscilloscope to the SYNC output of the 8080. Recall that the SYNC signal uniquely defines the beginning of each machine cycle (M cycle) of the 8080 but does not define an instruction cycle. How many M cycles does the 8080 use to execute a JMP instruction? See Pages 2-18 and 2-19 of the MCS-80 User's Manal.

1.3   Examine the system clocks with a 10X probe and compare the results with those of Experiment 9.

Step 2

We need to identify the beginning of the JMP instruction cycle. Referring to the status word chart (Appendix, Figure A-8), note that D5 of the status word is uniquely high during SYNC for a JMP instruction.

2.1   Place a 10X probe on Pin 4 of the 8080 (D5 output). Using a second probe (channel B), examine Pin 19 of the 8080 (SYNC output) and verify which M cycle is an instruction FETCH (first M cycle).

2.2   With the trigger signal still coming from the SYNC output, examine the rest of the data bus lines (D0-D4, D6-D7) of the 8080. Record these in Table 21-1A. Verify that the data (status word) is for an instruction FETCH = 10100010_2.

2.3 Similarly, probe the address lines and record the

146

TABLE 21-1   Logic levels of the data and address buses while the 8080 is running

	BUS NAME	\multicolumn{16}{c}{BIT NUMBER}
		0	1	2	3	4	5	6	7	8	9	10	11	12	13	14	15
(A)	DATA (STATUS WORD)																
(B)	ADDRESS																
(C)	DATA																
	NOTES:																

results in Table 21-1B. Verify that the address bus is equal to the memory location where the JMP instruction OP-CODE was stored in Step 1.1.

Step 3

Lastly, verify the status words for the remaining two M cycles of the jump instruction.

3.1   Trigger on the sync signal and identify the first M cycle as was done in Step 2.1.

3.2   Display all three M cycles on the oscilloscope screen by selecting an appropriate sweep speed.

3.3   Examine the data bus signals during the SYNC signal of M2 and M3 and record them in Table 21-1C.

3.4   Verify that the status words correspond to a memory read (status word = 82_{16}).

147

QUESTIONS

    1.   Why are microprocessor signals difficult to analyze with an oscilloscope?

    2.   What is an advantage of using an oscilloscope in troubleshooting a microprocessor system?

    3.   What signal(s) could be used to define uniquely the second M cycle of the following instructions:

        IN   MOV   PUSH

        OUT   CALL

    4.   When is the program counter incremented during the instructions listed in Question 3? Answer in terms of which M cycle(s).

    5.   Draw a schematic for a simple trigger circuit that could be used in identifying M1 of any instruction cycle.

APPENDIX A
**CMS SYSTEM SCHEMATICS
AND BLOCK DIAGRAMS**

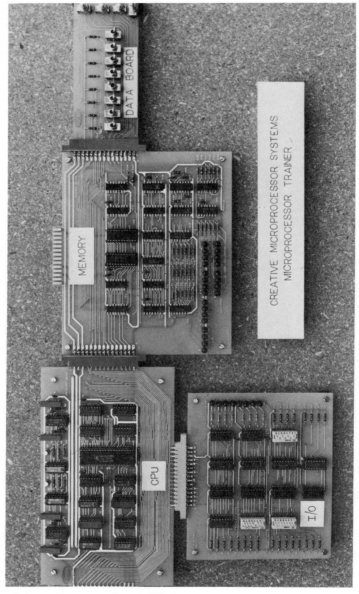

© Creative Microprocessor Systems, 1979

FIGURE A-1   Photograph of Creative Microprocessor Systems' 8080 hardware
training system with the Static Stimulus Tester connected

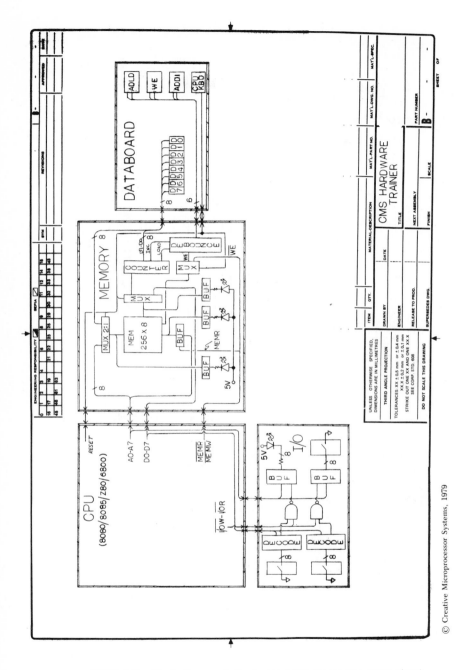

FIGURE A-2   Block diagram of the Creative Microprocessor Systems(CMS)
hardware training system

151

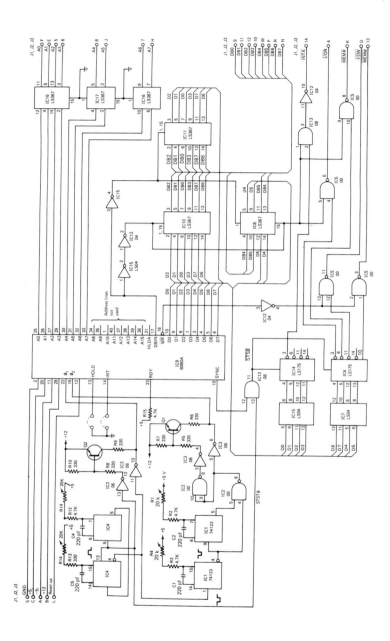

FIGURE A-3A   Schematic diagram of the 8080 CPU board in the CMS hardware
training system

152

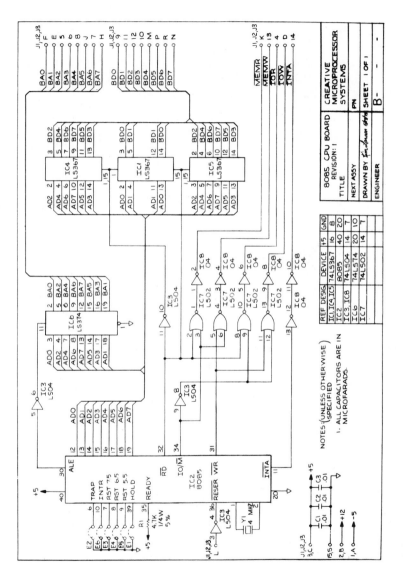

FIGURE A-3B   Schematic diagram of the 8085 CPU board in the CMS hardware
training system

© Creative Microprocessor Systems, 1979

153

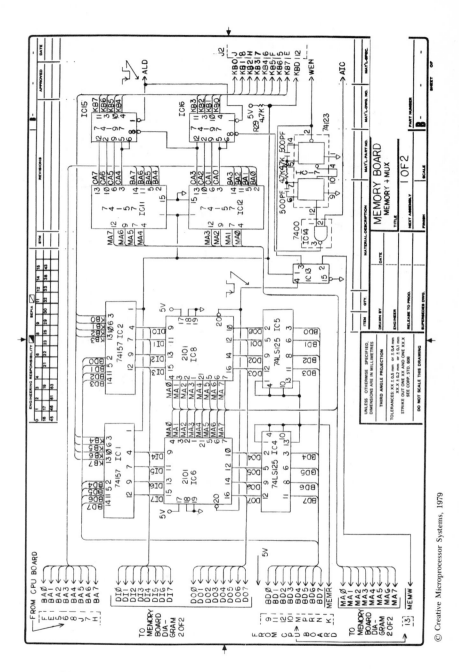

FIGURE A-4A   Partial schematic diagram of the Memory board in the CMS
hardware training system (memory ICs and multiplexers)

© Creative Microprocessor Systems, 1979

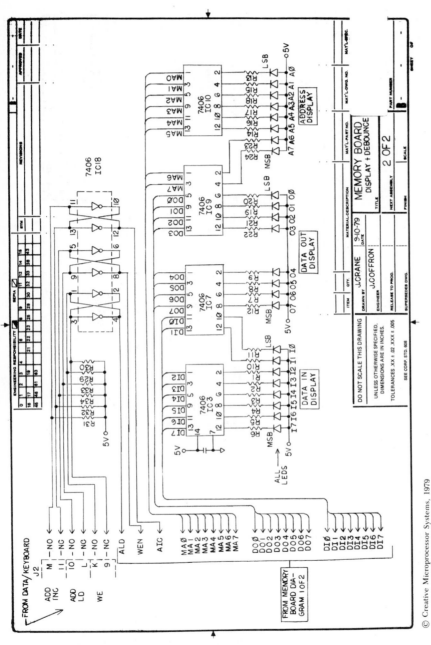

FIGURE A-4B   Partial schematic diagram of the Memory board in the CMS
hardware training system (display and debounce circuitry)

155

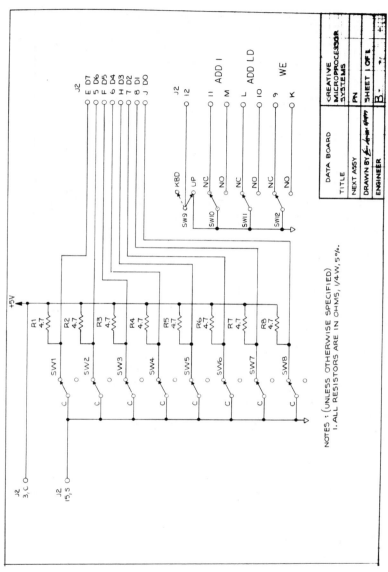

FIGURE A-5   Schematic diagram of the Data board in the CMS hardware training system

156

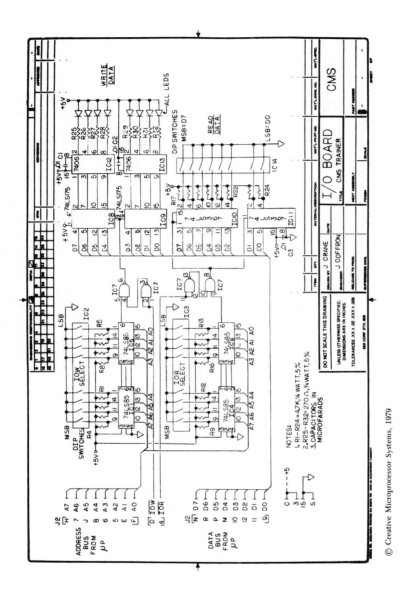

FIGURE A-6   Schematic diagram of the I/O board in the CMS hardware training
system

157

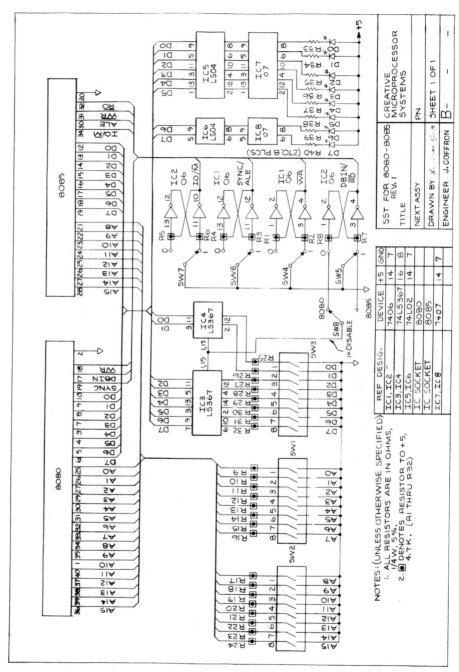

FIGURE A-7   Schematic diagram of the Static Stimulus Tester (SST) used with
8080 and 8085 systems

158

Instructions for the 8080 require from one to five machine cycles for complete execution. The 8080 sends out 8 bit of status information on the data bus at the beginning of each machine cycle (during SYNC time). The following table defines the status information.

STATUS INFORMATION DEFINITION

Symbols	Data Bus Bit	Definition
INTA*	D_0	Acknowledge signal for INTERRUPT request. Signal should be used to gate a restart instruction onto the data bus when DBIN is active.
$\overline{WO}$	D_1	Indicates that the operation in the current machine cycle will be a WRITE memory or OUTPUT function ($\overline{WO}$ = 0). Otherwise, a READ memory or INPUT operation will be executed.
STACK	D_2	Indicates that the address bus holds the pushdown stack address from the Stack Pointer.
HLTA	D_3	Acknowledge signal for HALT instruction.
OUT	D_4	Indicates that the address bus contains the address of an output device and the data bus will contain the output data when $\overline{WR}$ is active.
M_1	D_5	Provides a signal to indicate that the CPU is in the fetch cycle for the first byte of an instruction.
INP*	D_6	Indicates that the address bus contains the address of an input device and the input data should be placed on the data bus when DBIN is active.
MEMR*	D_7	Designates that the data bus will be used for memory read data.

*These three status bits can be used to control the flow of data onto the 8080 data bus.

STATUS WORD CHART

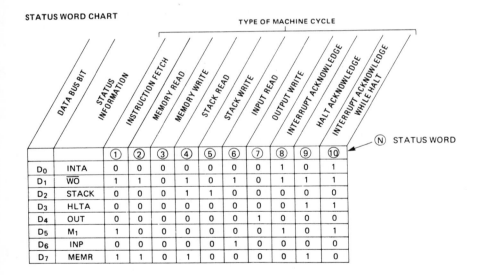

Data Bus Bit	Status Information	Instruction Fetch ①	Memory Read ②	Memory Write ③	Stack Read ④	Stack Write ⑤	Input Read ⑥	Output Write ⑦	Interrupt Acknowledge ⑧	Halt Acknowledge ⑨	Interrupt Acknowledge While Halt ⑩
D_0	INTA	0	0	0	0	0	0	0	1	0	1
D_1	$\overline{WO}$	1	1	0	1	0	1	0	1	1	1
D_2	STACK	0	0	0	1	1	0	0	0	0	0
D_3	HLTA	0	0	0	0	0	0	0	0	1	1
D_4	OUT	0	0	0	0	0	0	1	0	0	0
D_5	M_1	1	0	0	0	0	0	0	1	0	1
D_6	INP	0	0	0	0	0	1	0	0	0	0
D_7	MEMR	1	1	0	1	0	0	0	0	1	0

FIGURE A-8   Summary of the Status Word output by the 8080 microprocessor

159